I'm in the garden bring more wine
Wine
Garden
vintage wine Garden
wine o' clock

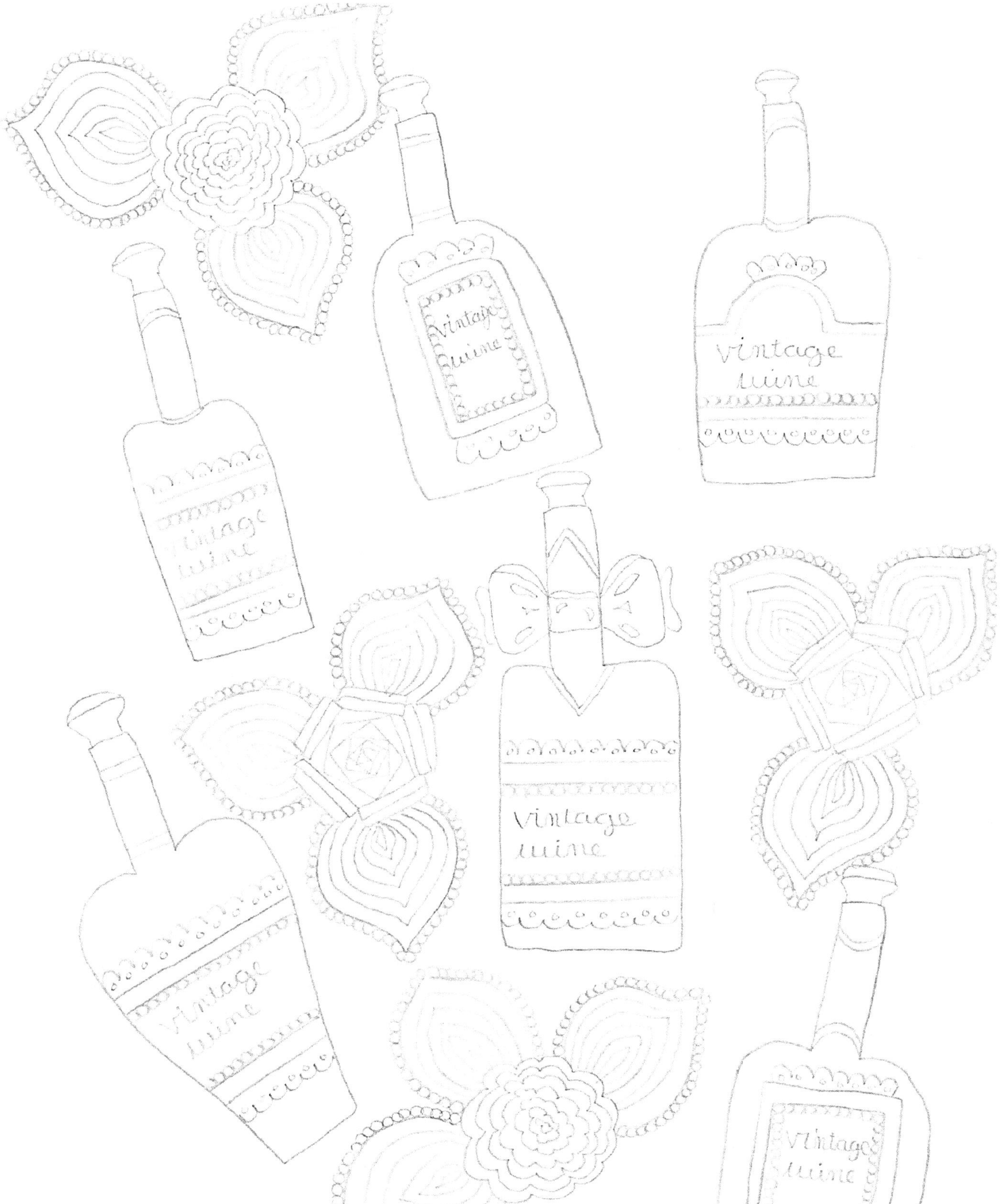
Vintage wine
Vintage wine
Vintage wine
Vintage wine
Vintage wine
Vintage wine

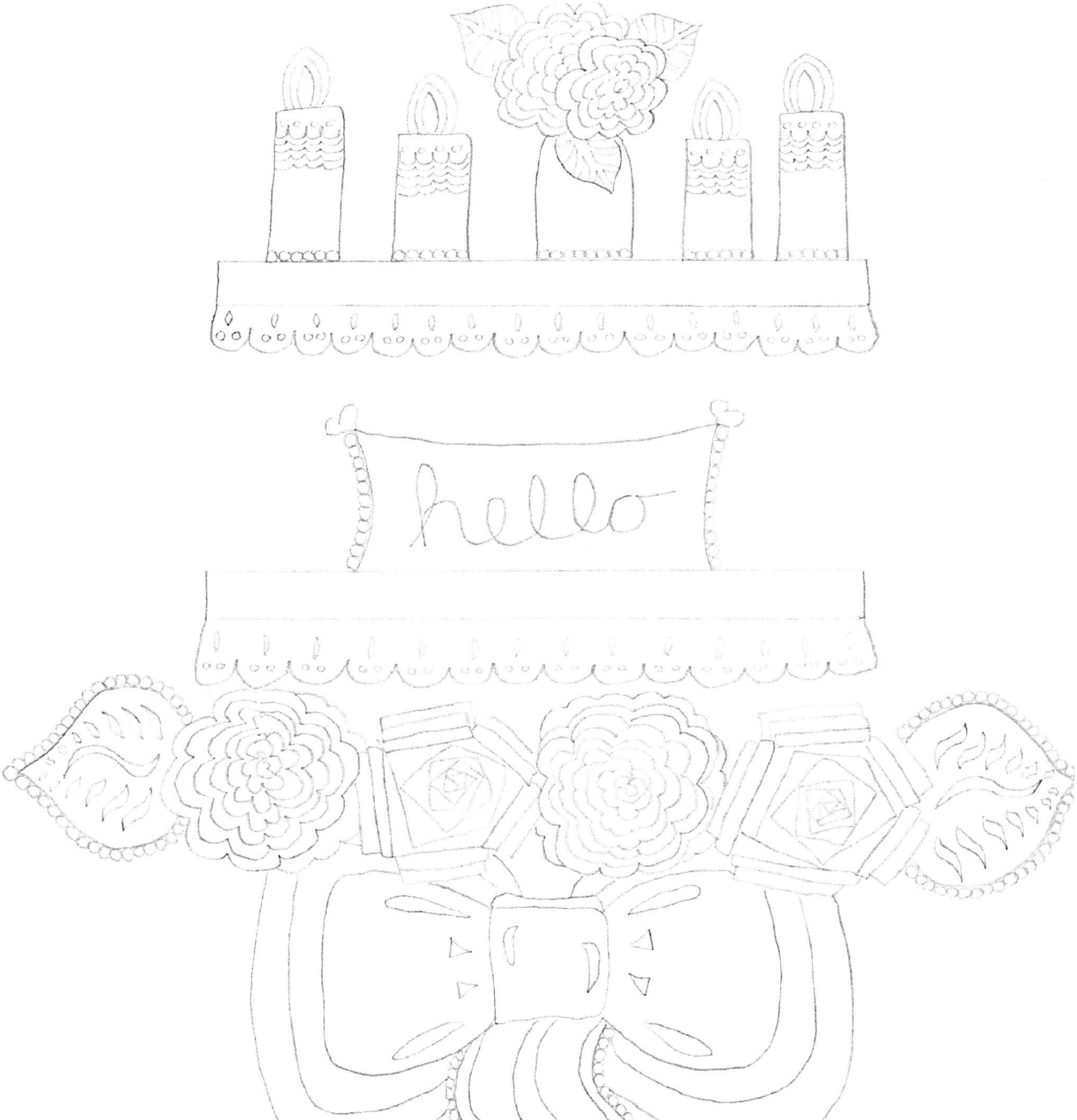
hello

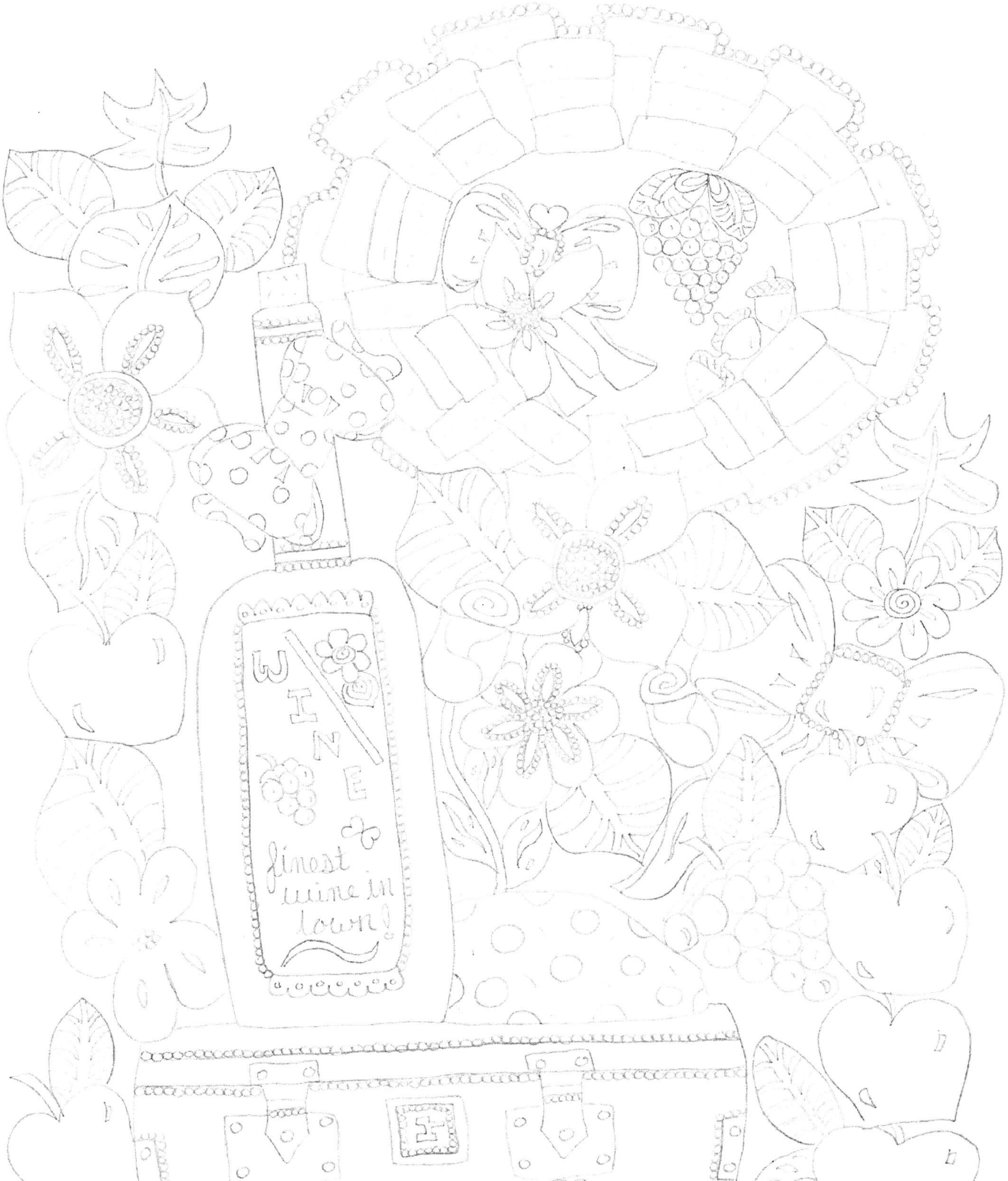
WINE
finest wine in town!

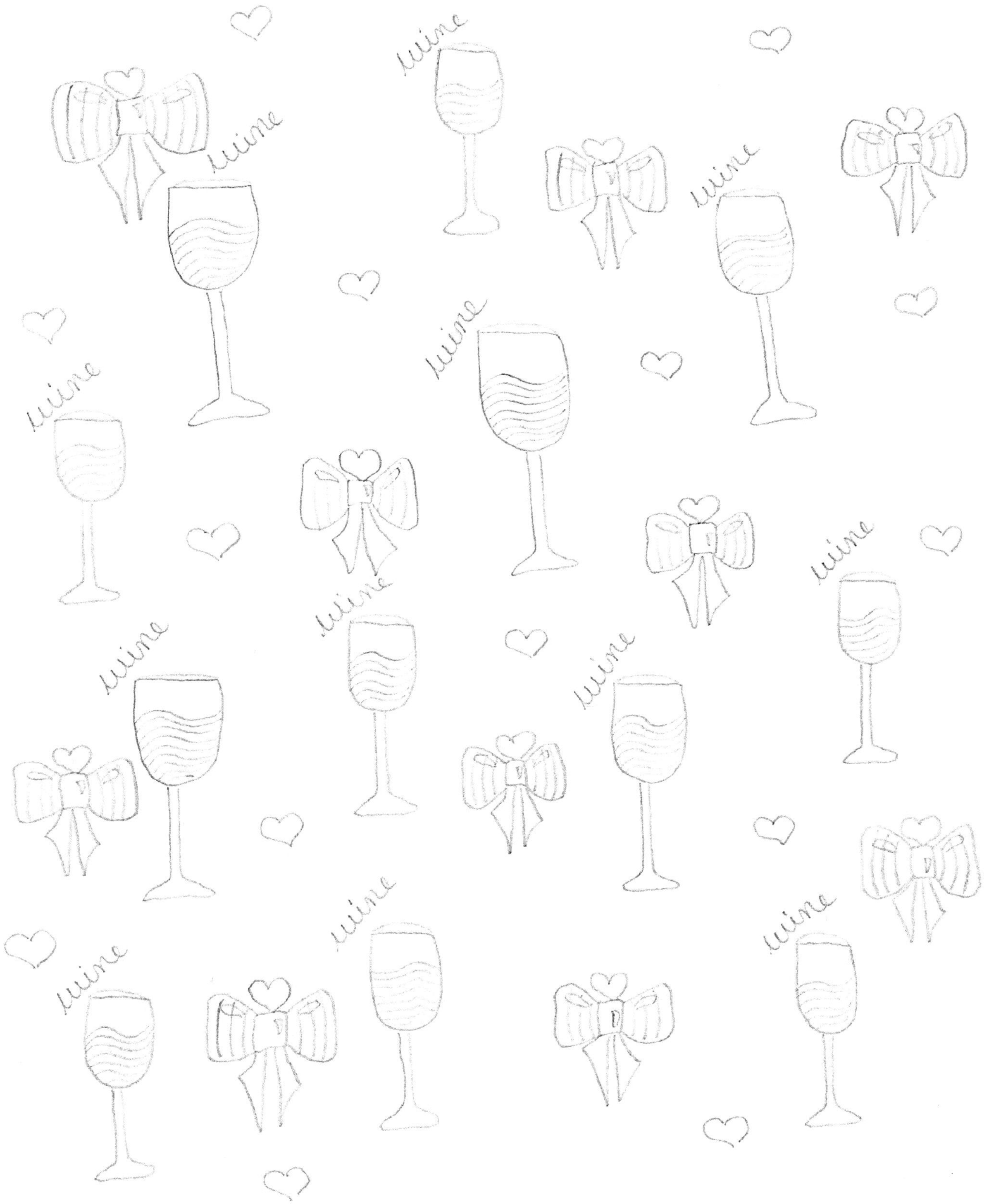
wine
wine
wine
wine
wine
wine
wine
wine
wine
wine
wine
wine

Live
Laugh
Wine

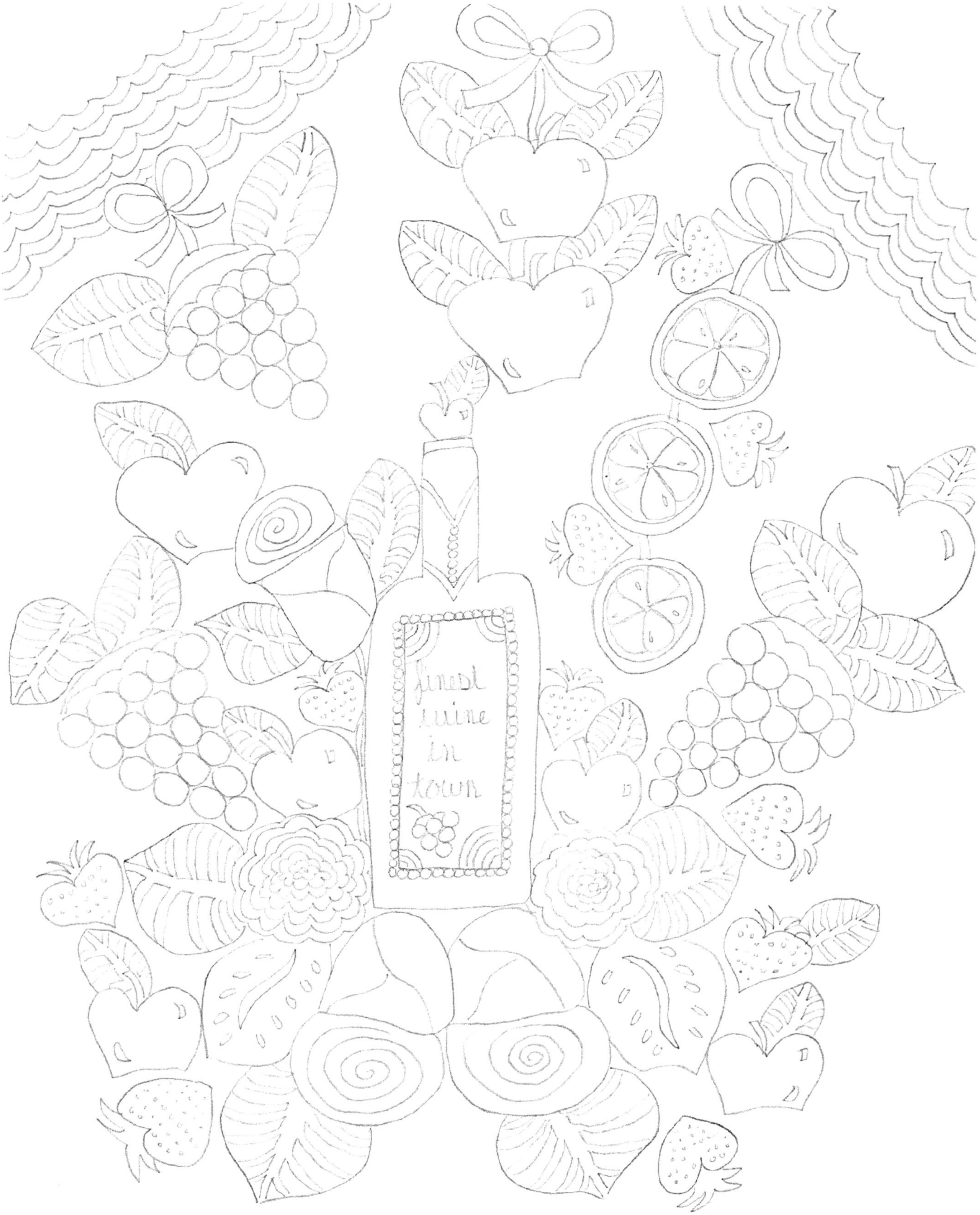
finest
wine
in
town

wine

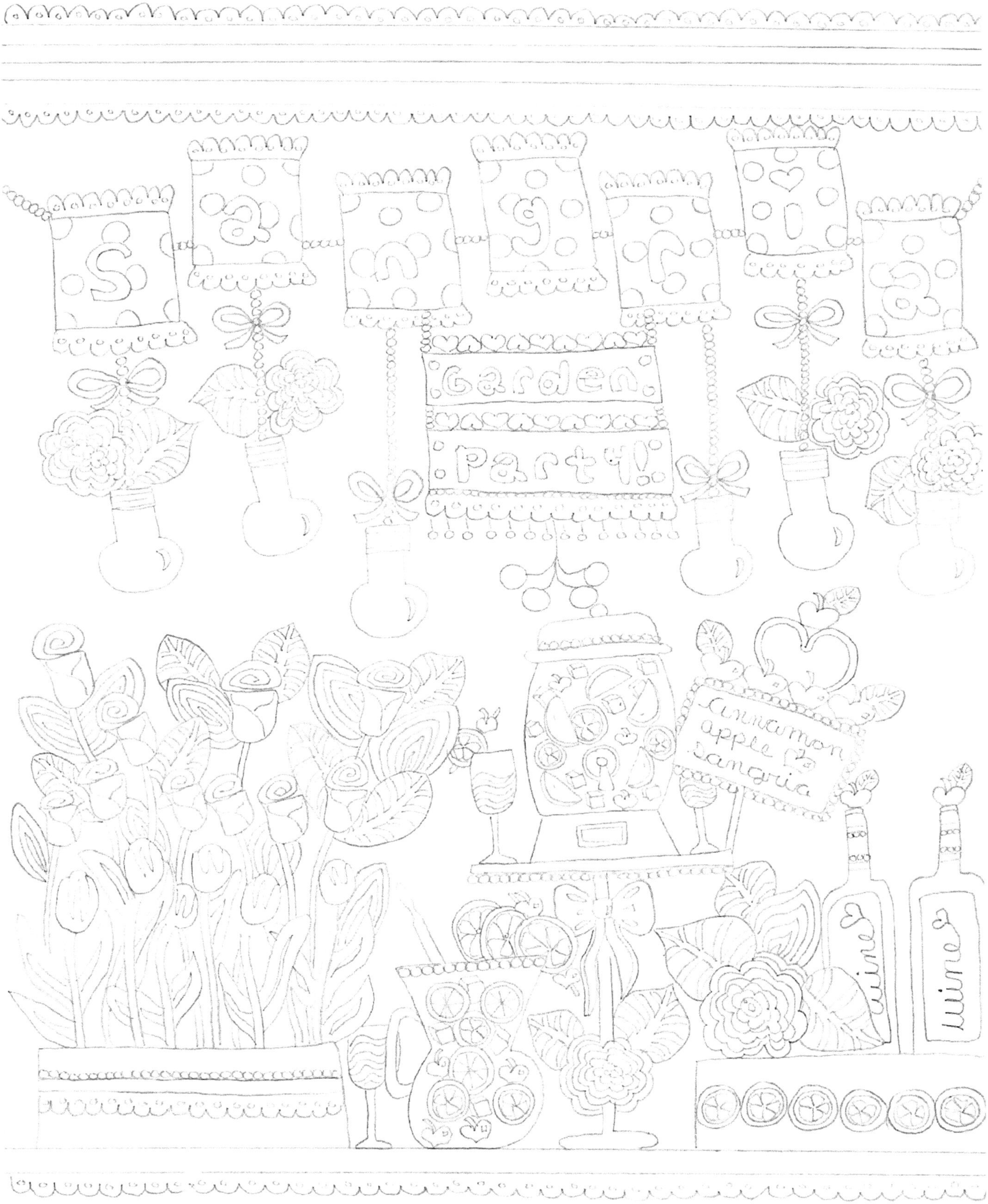
Sangria
Garden Party!
Cinnamon apple Sangria
wine
wine

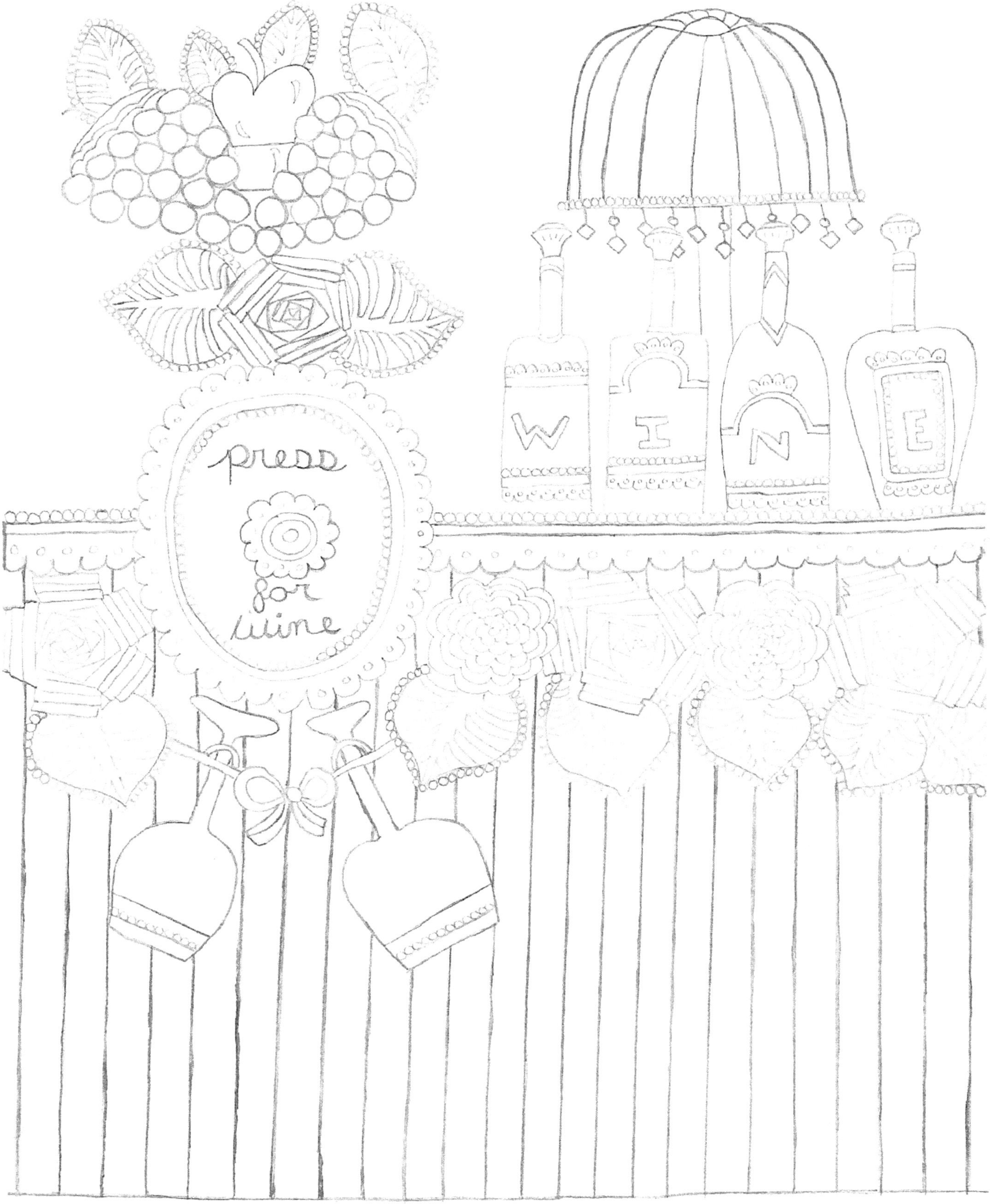
press
for
wine
W
I
N
E

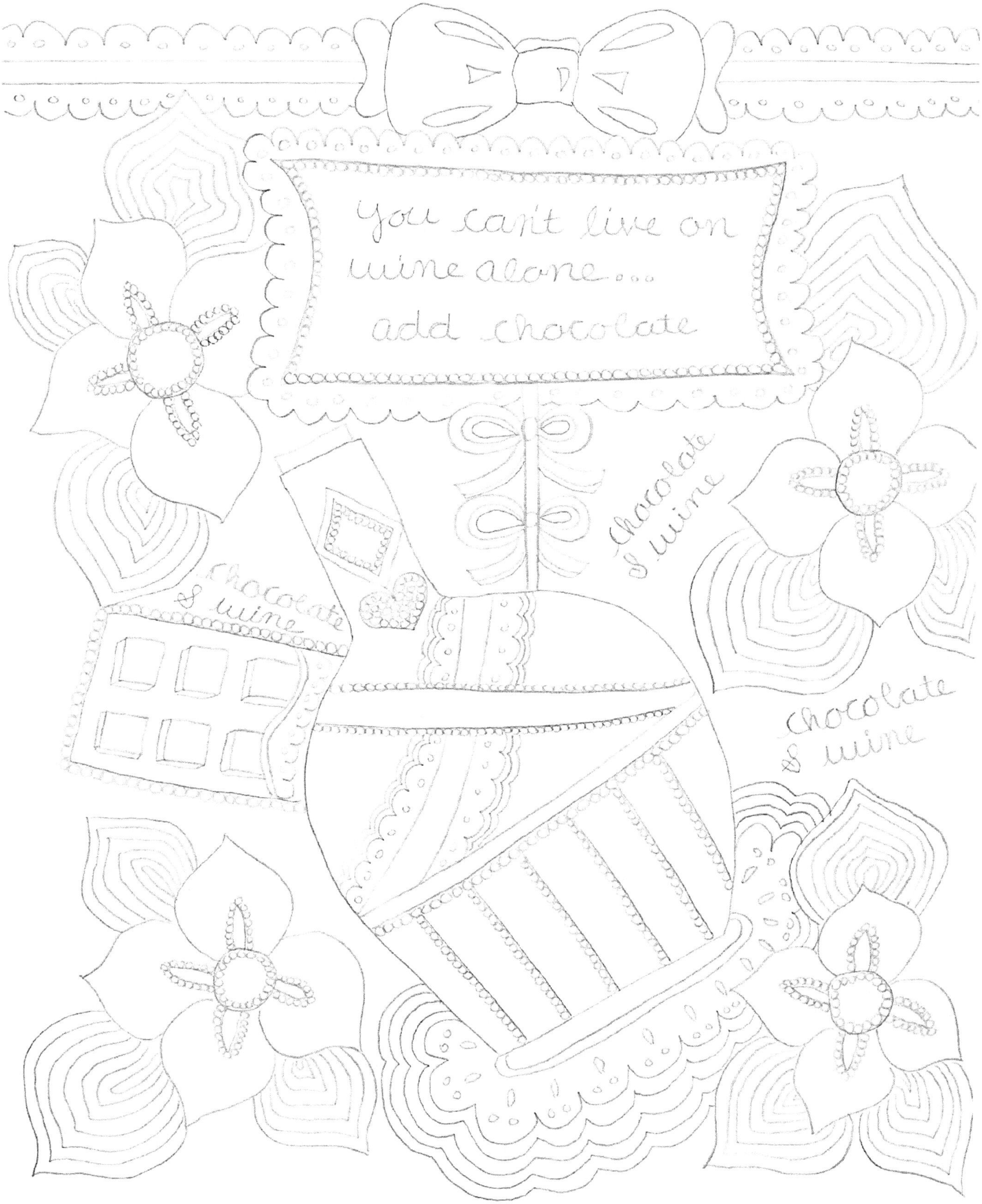
You can't live on wine alone... add chocolate
Chocolate & wine
Chocolate & wine
Chocolate & wine

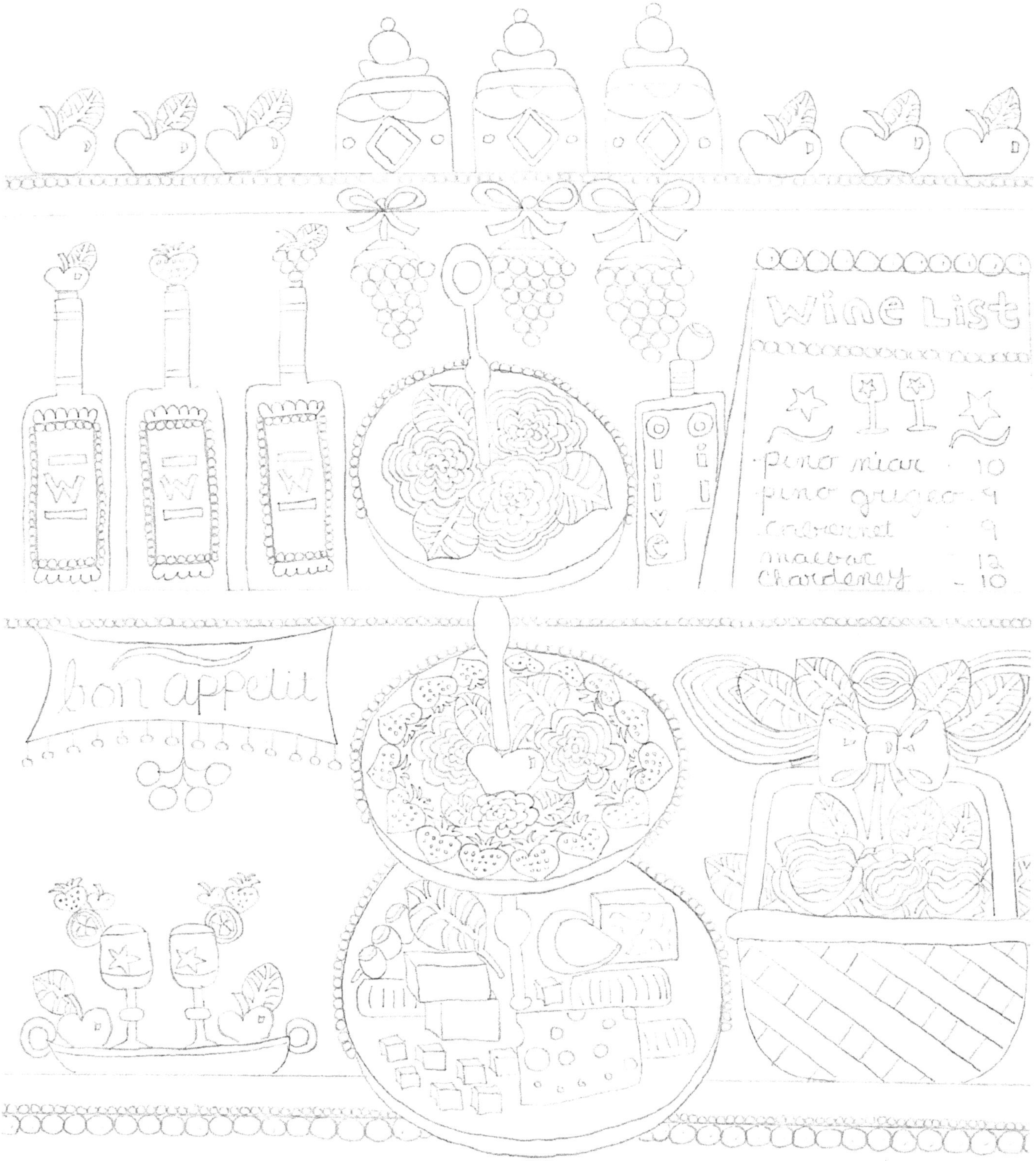
Wine List
pino niar 10
pino grigeo 9
Cabernet 9
malbac 12
Chardoney - 10
bon appetit

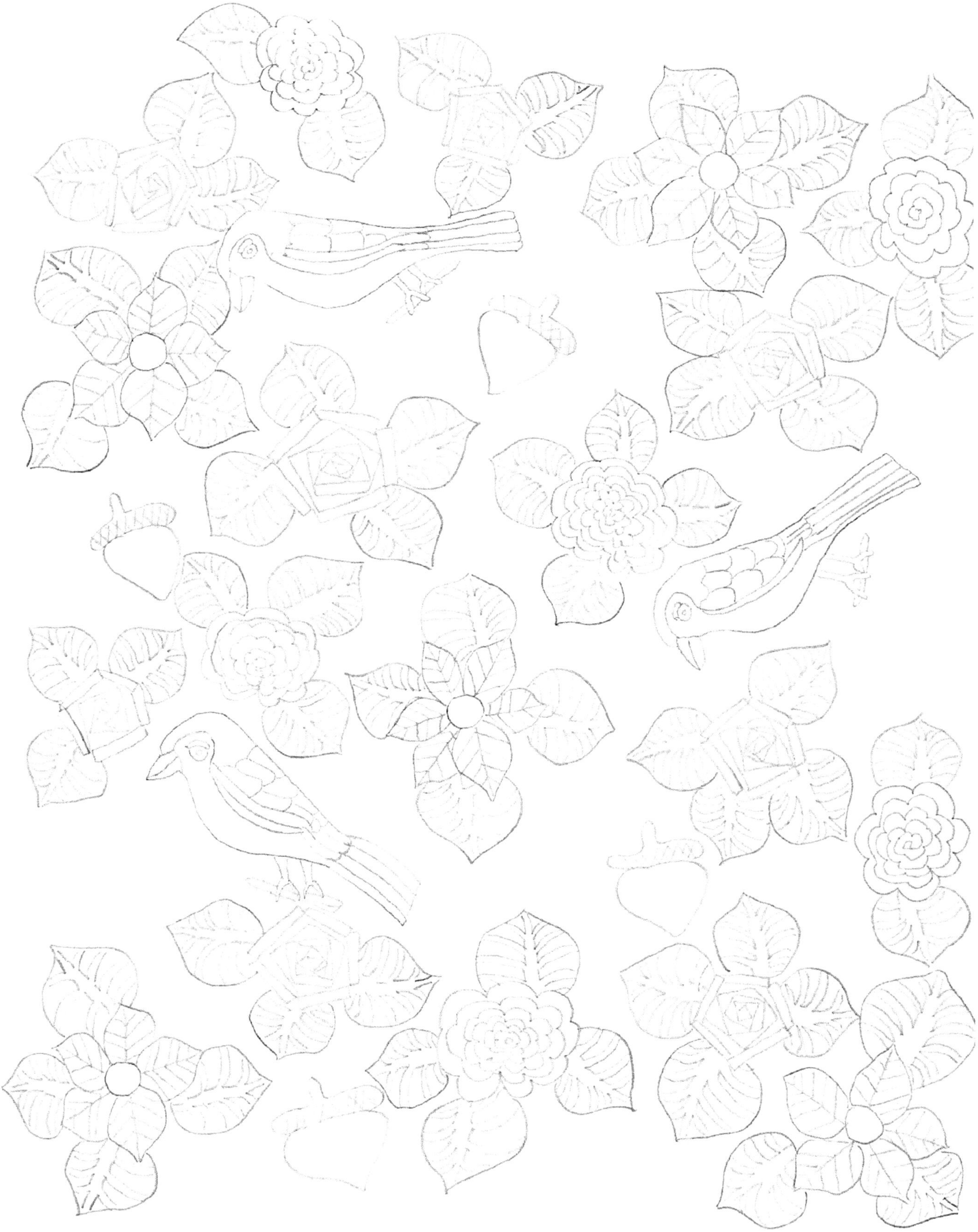

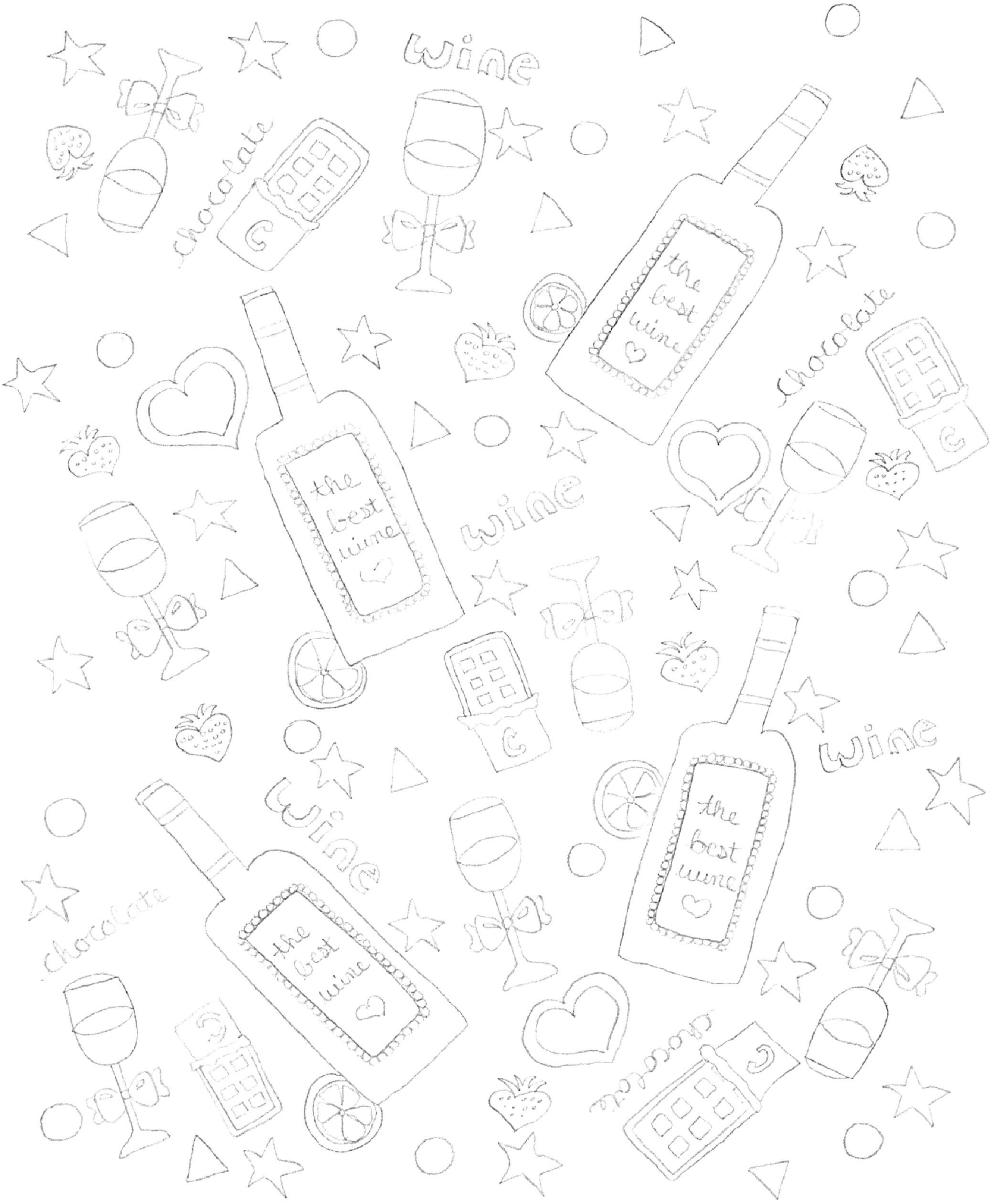
wine
chocolate
the best wine
chocolate
wine
the best wine
wine
the best wine
chocolate
wine
the best wine
chocolate

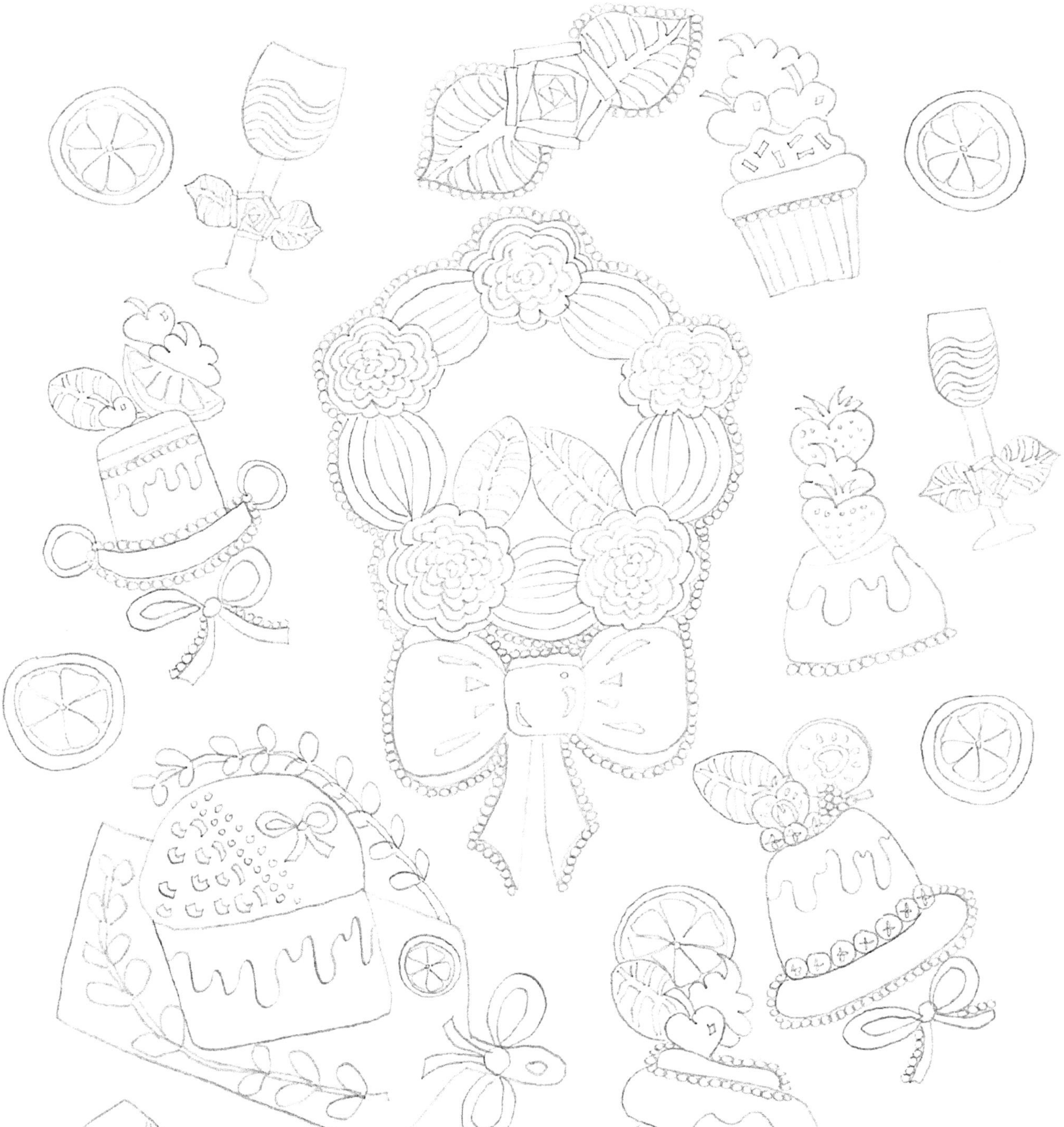

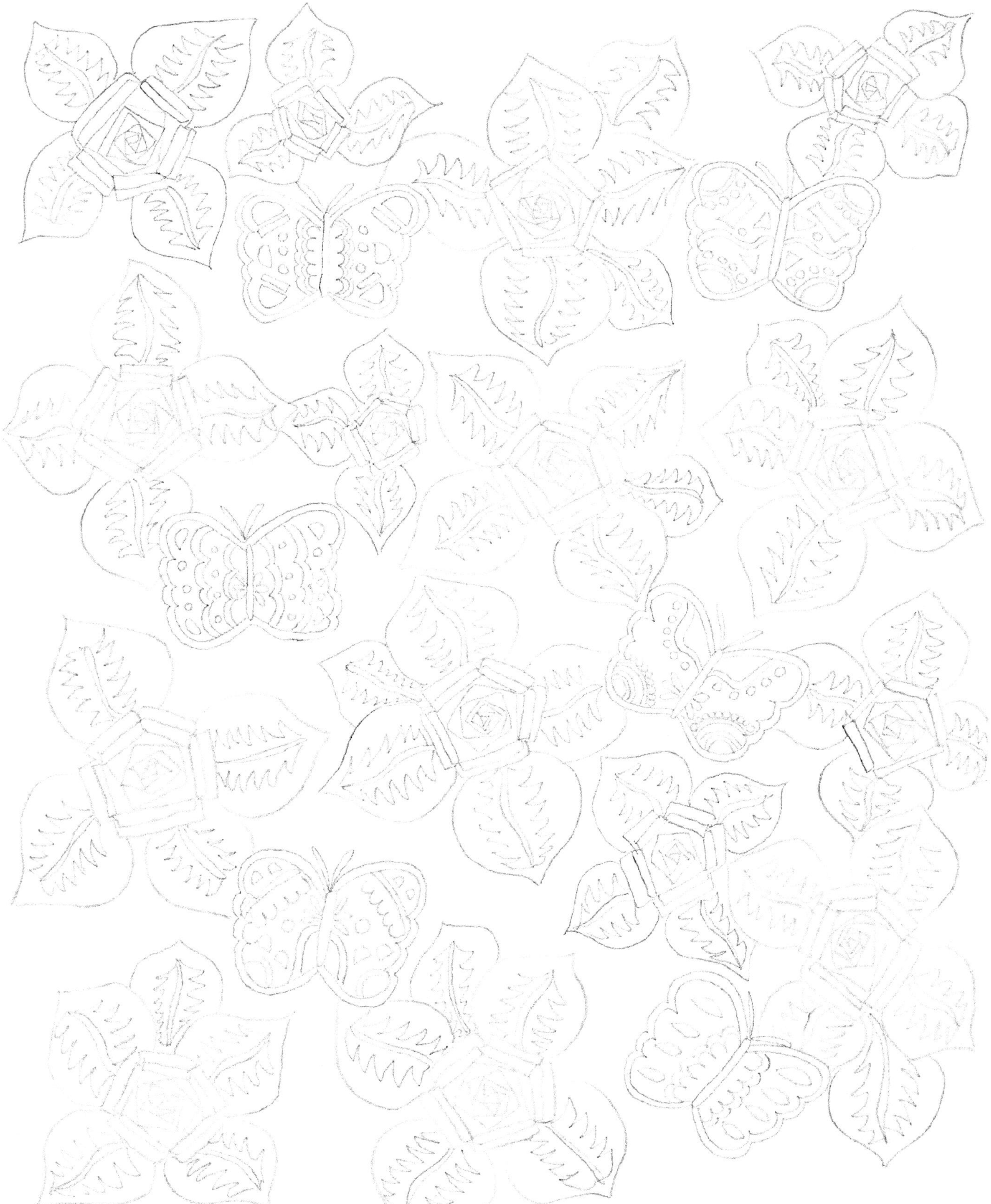

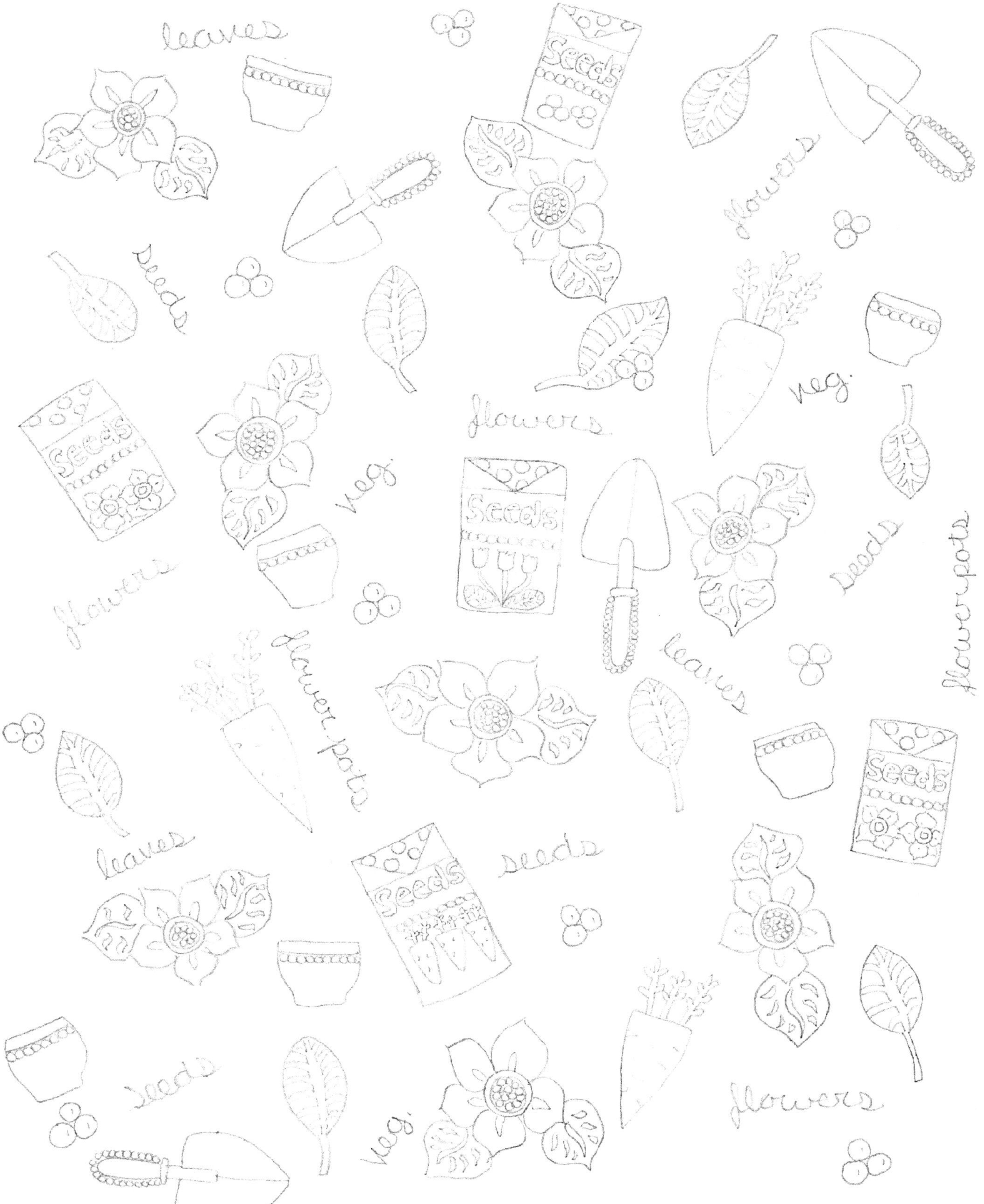
leaves
Seeds
flowers
seeds
flowers
veg.
Seeds
veg.
Seeds
seeds
flower pots
flowers
flower pots
leaves
Seeds
leaves
Seeds
seeds
seeds
veg.
flowers

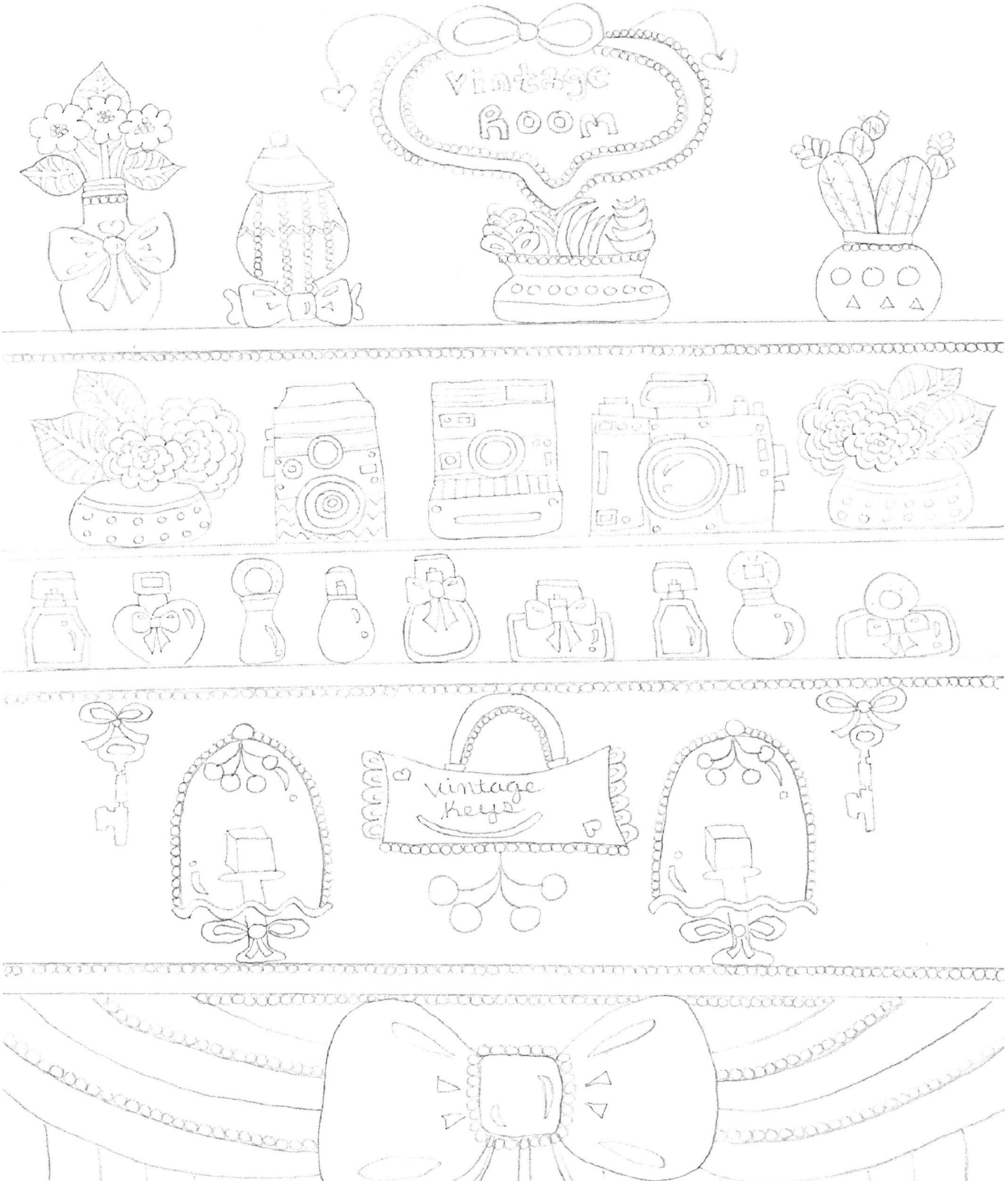
Vintage Room
Vintage Keys

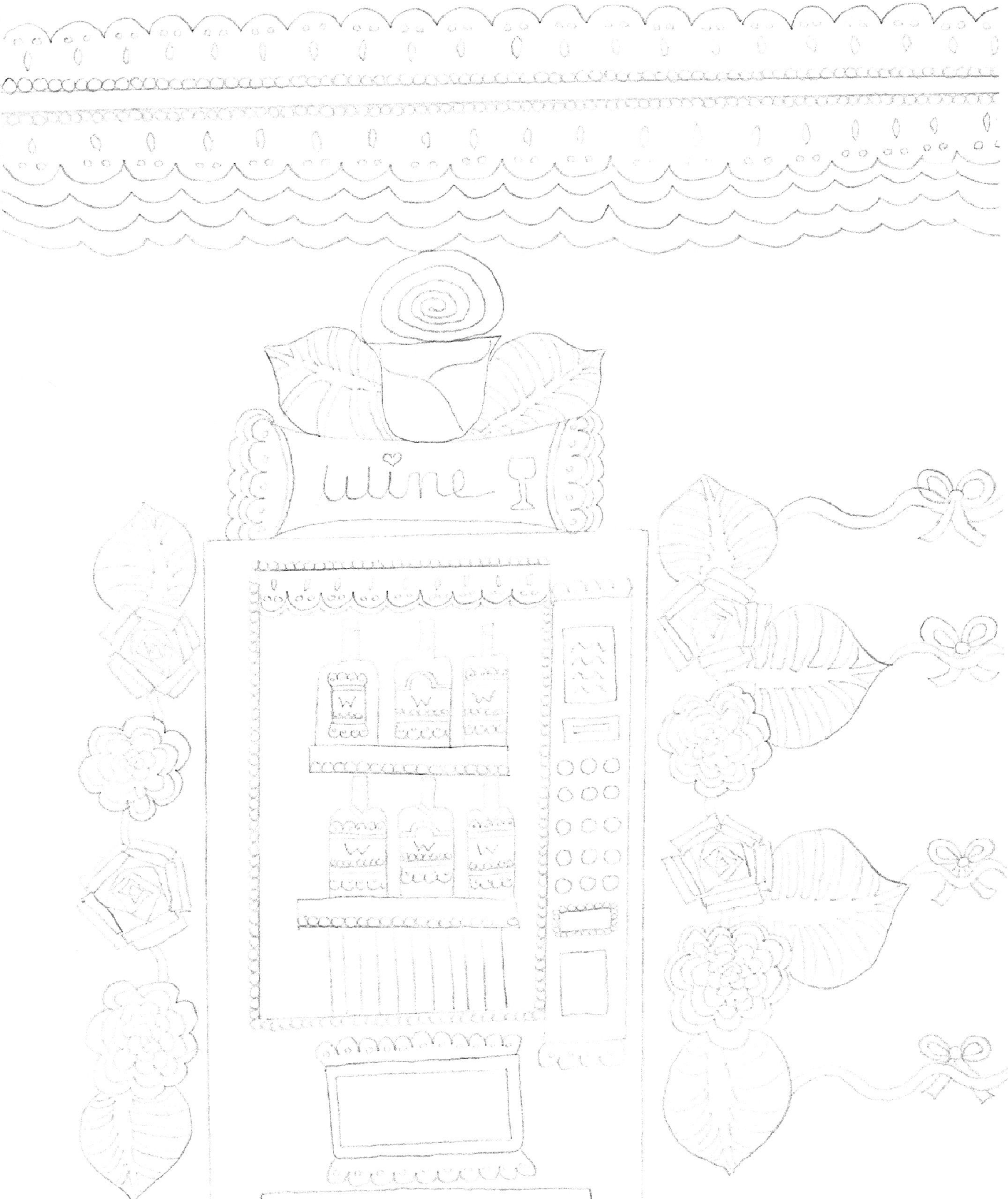
wine

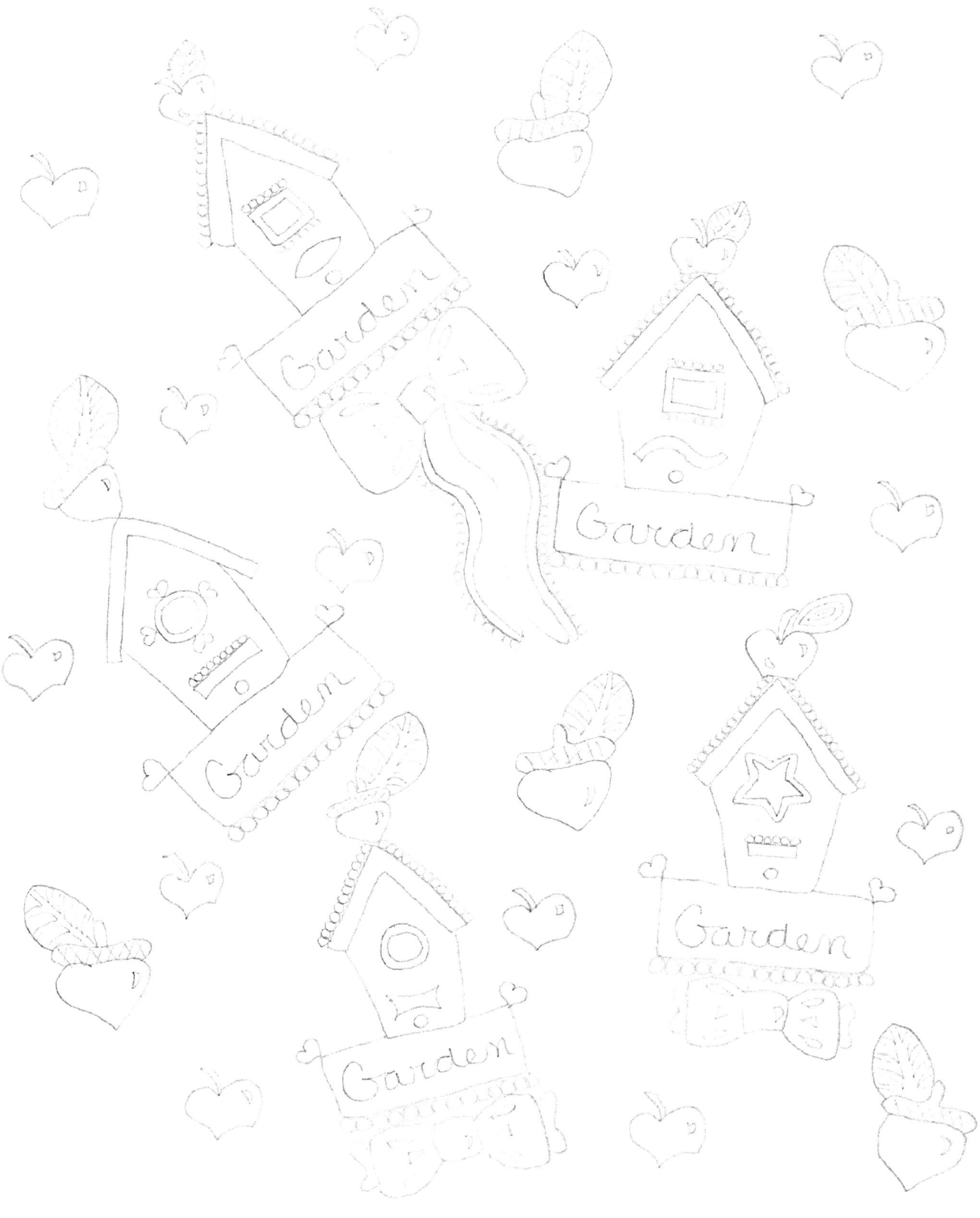
Garden
Garden
Garden
Garden
Garden

Apple Jam
It's wine Time!

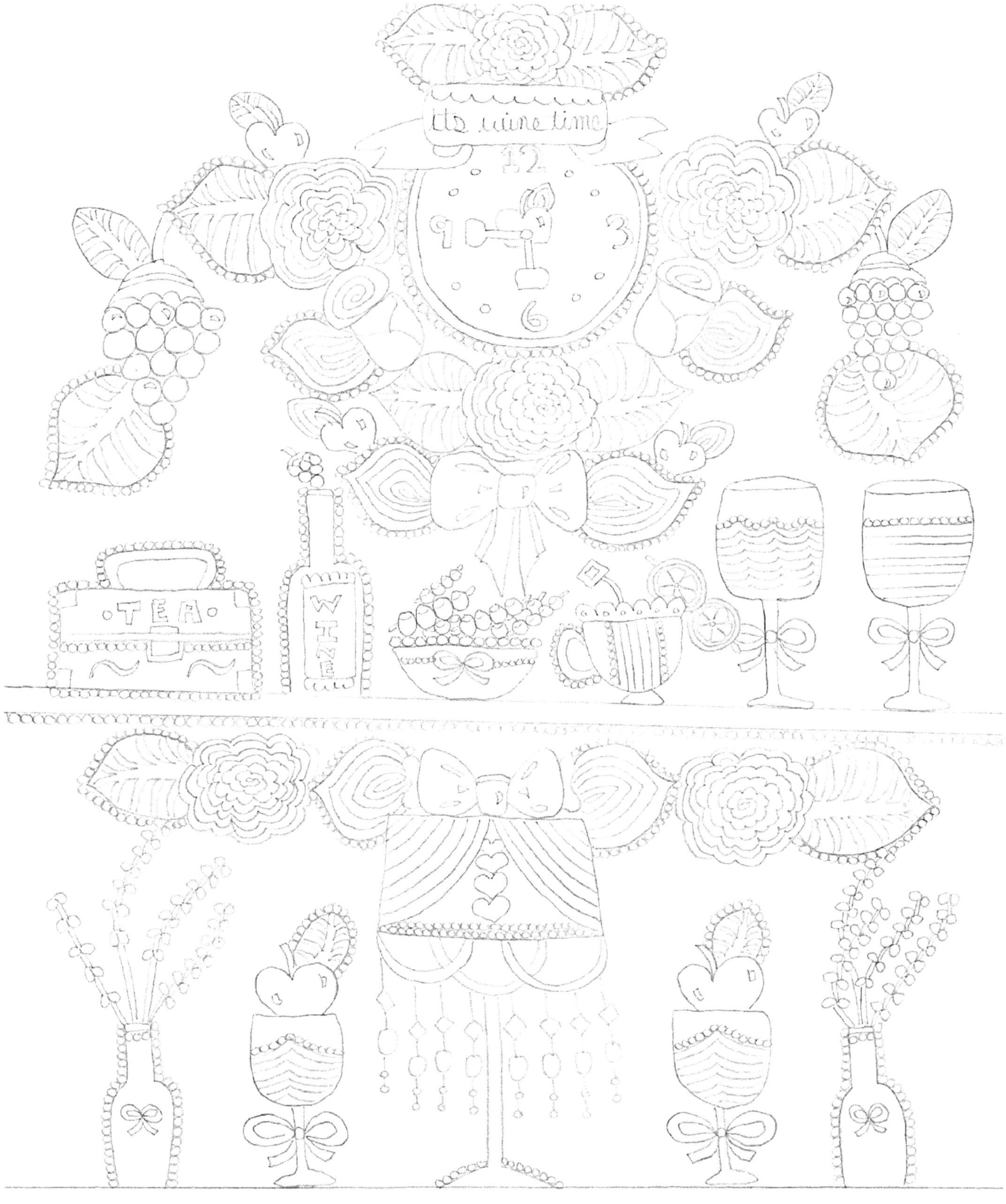
its wine time
12
9
3
6
TEA
WINE

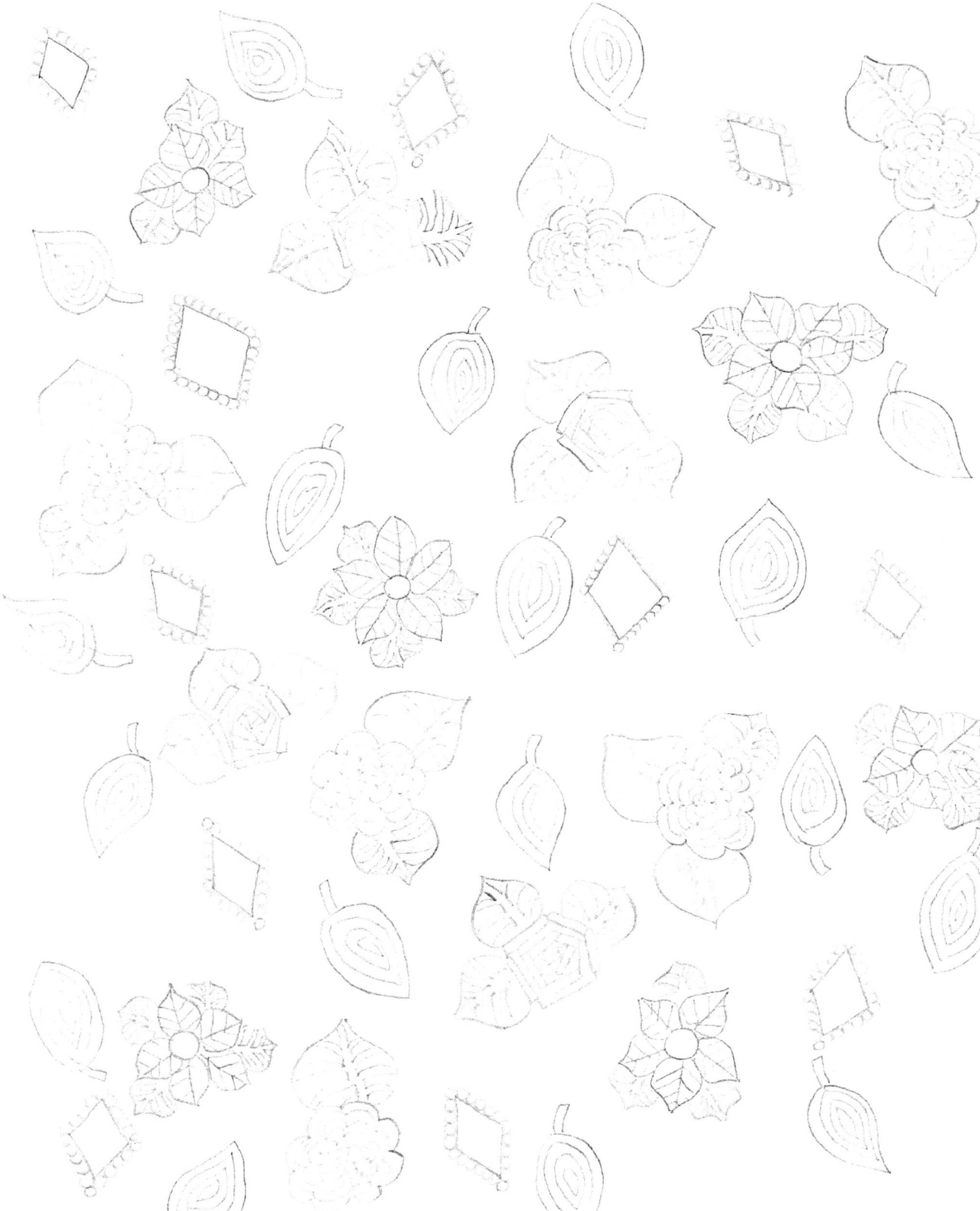

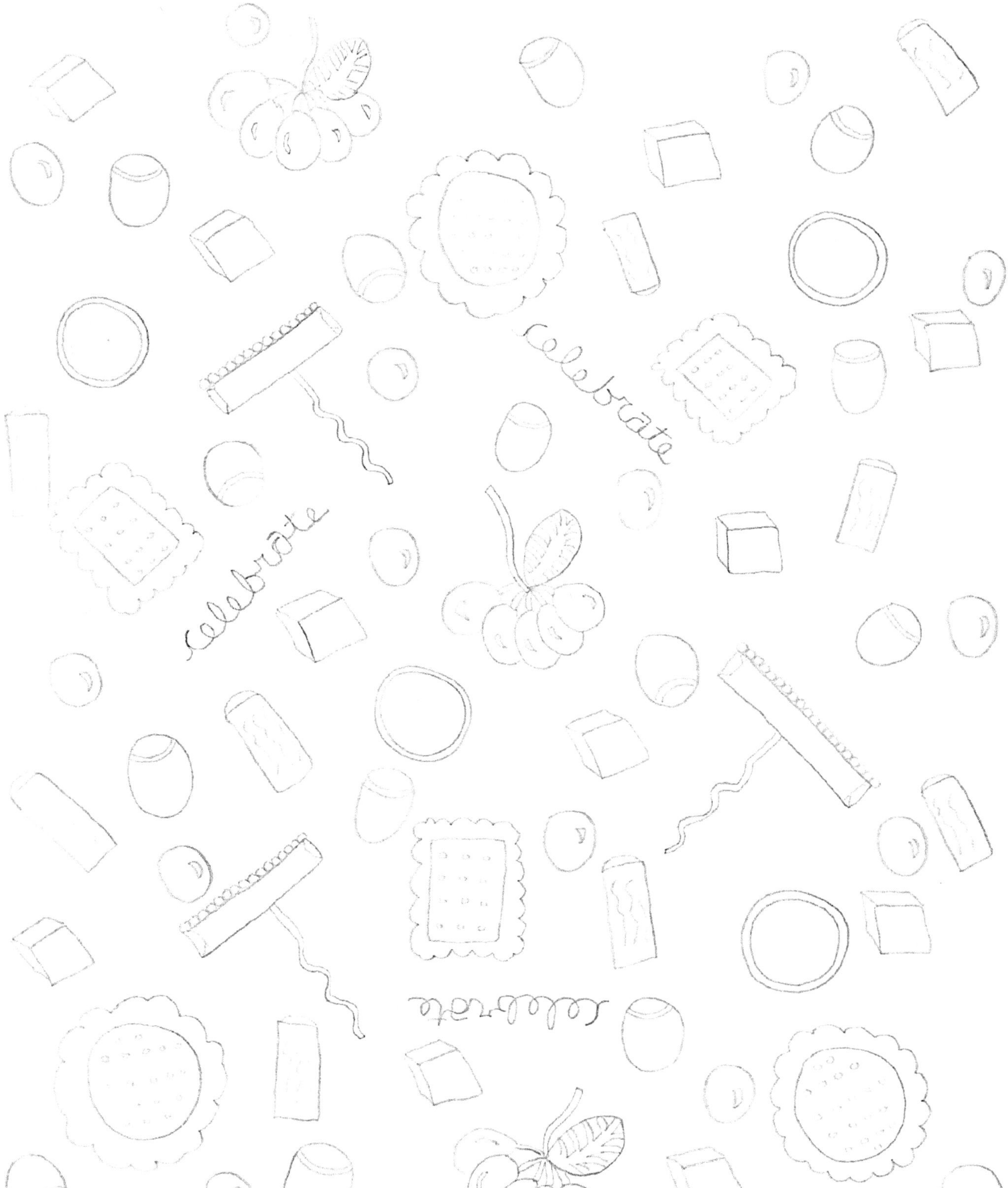
celebrate
celebrate
celebrate
celebrate

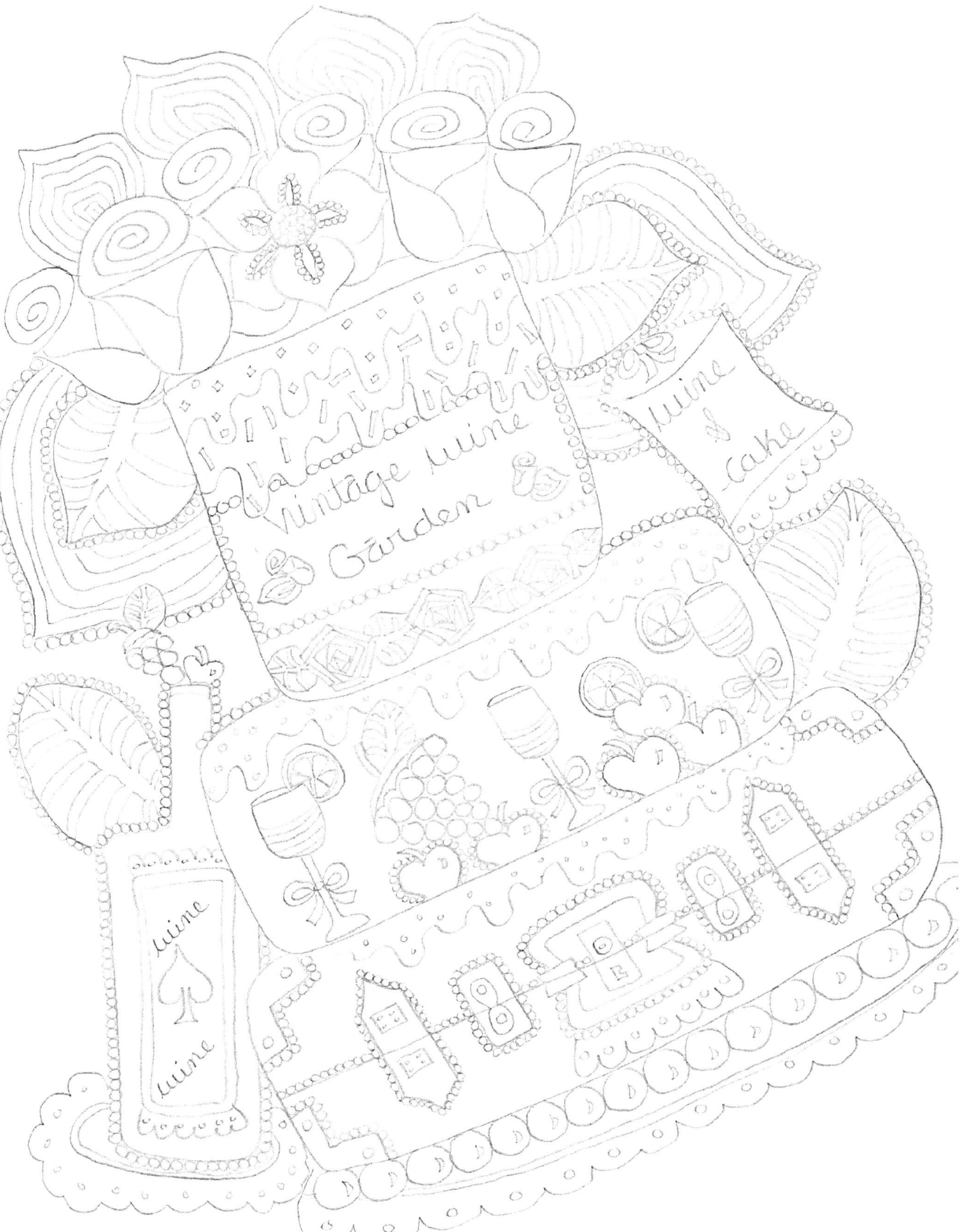

Vintage Wine Garden
wine & cake
wine
wine

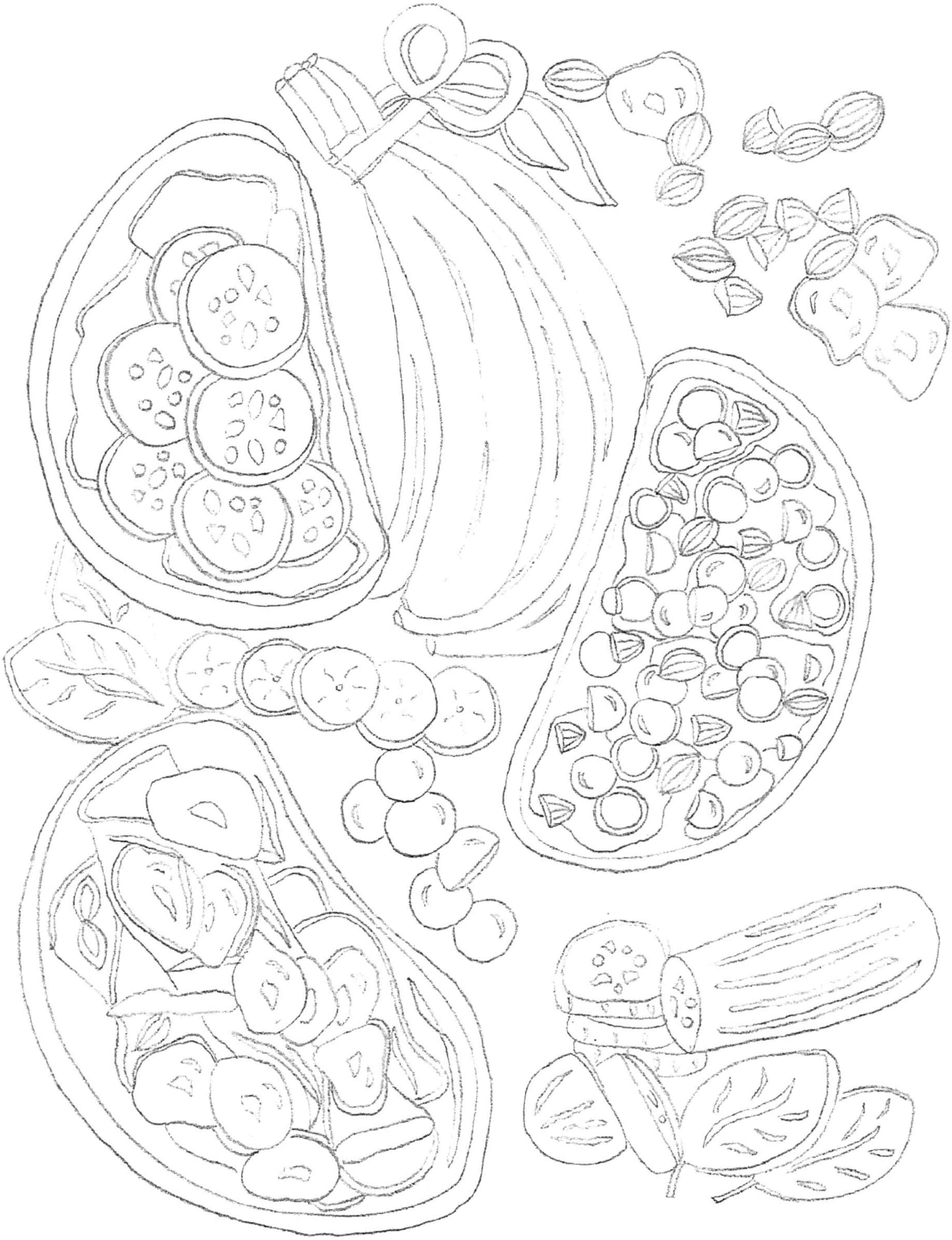

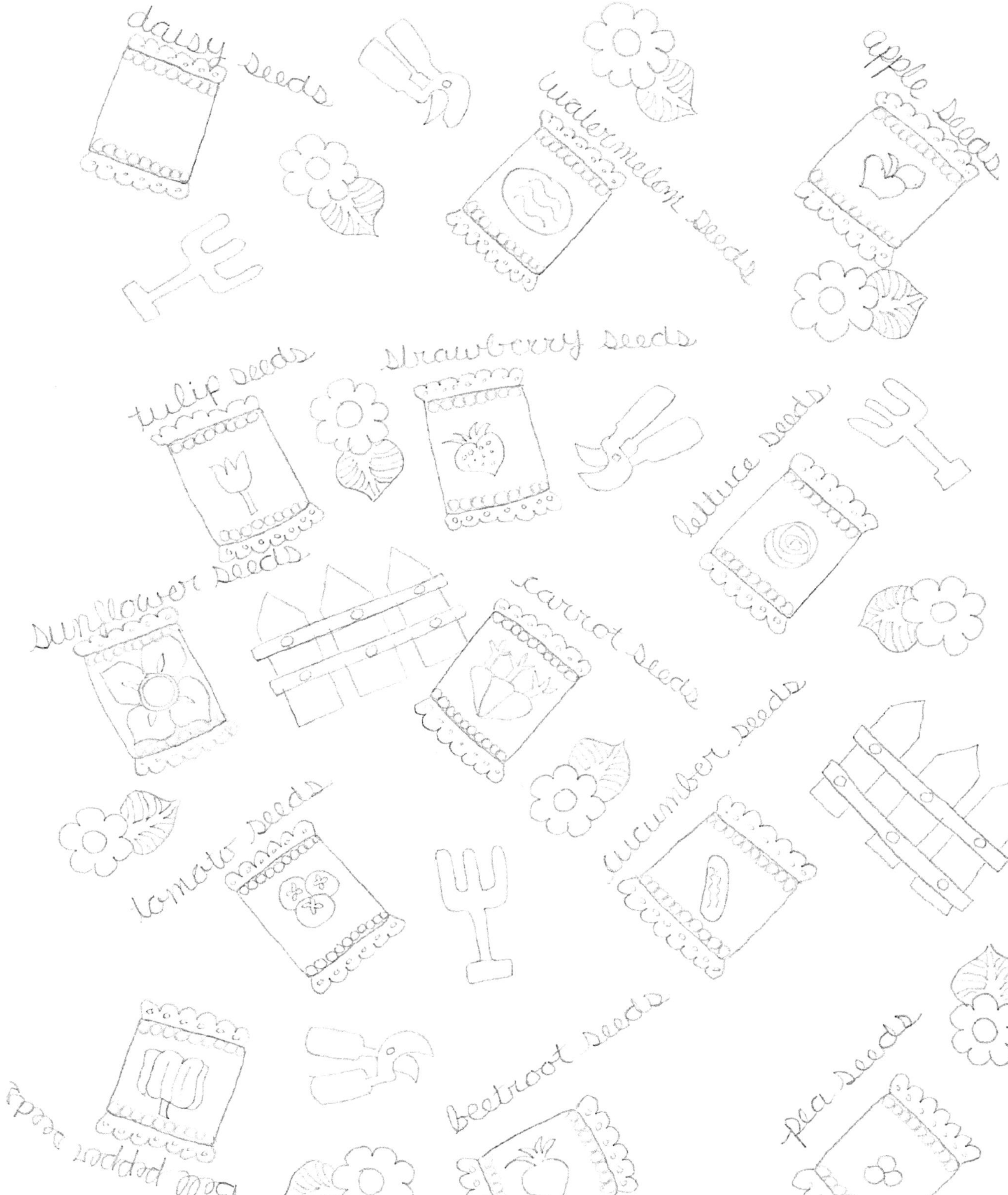
daisy seeds
apple seeds
watermelon seeds
strawberry seeds
tulip seeds
lettuce seeds
sunflower seeds
carrot seeds
cucumber seeds
tomato seeds
beetroot seeds
pea seeds
Bell pepper seeds

white wine
Vintage
Wine
Garden
Sangria
Red wine
Spritzer
Sangria

vintage wine Garden
Wine Time.
red wine tea
Wine O'clock
The Winery
white wine tea

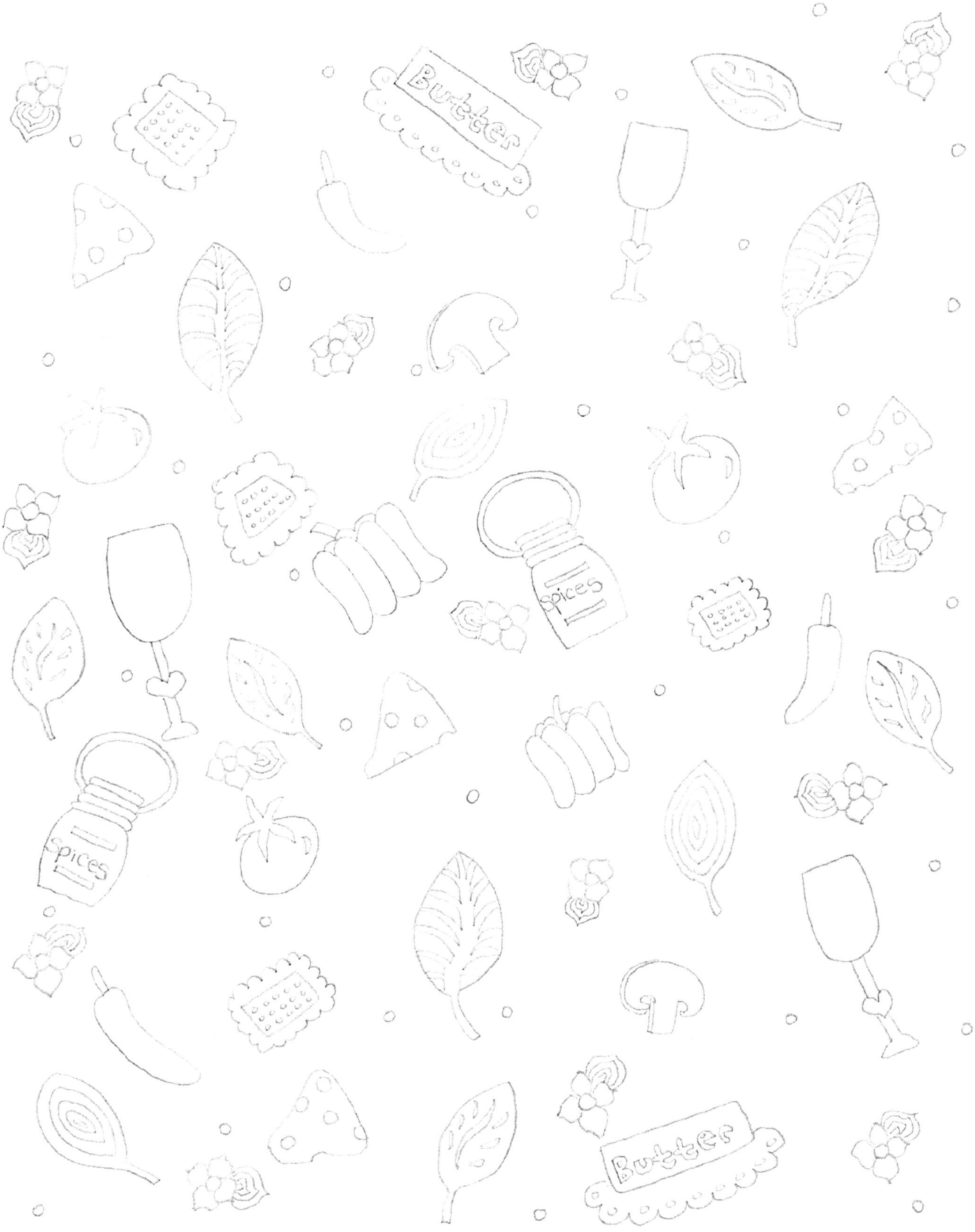
Butter
Spices
Spices
Butter

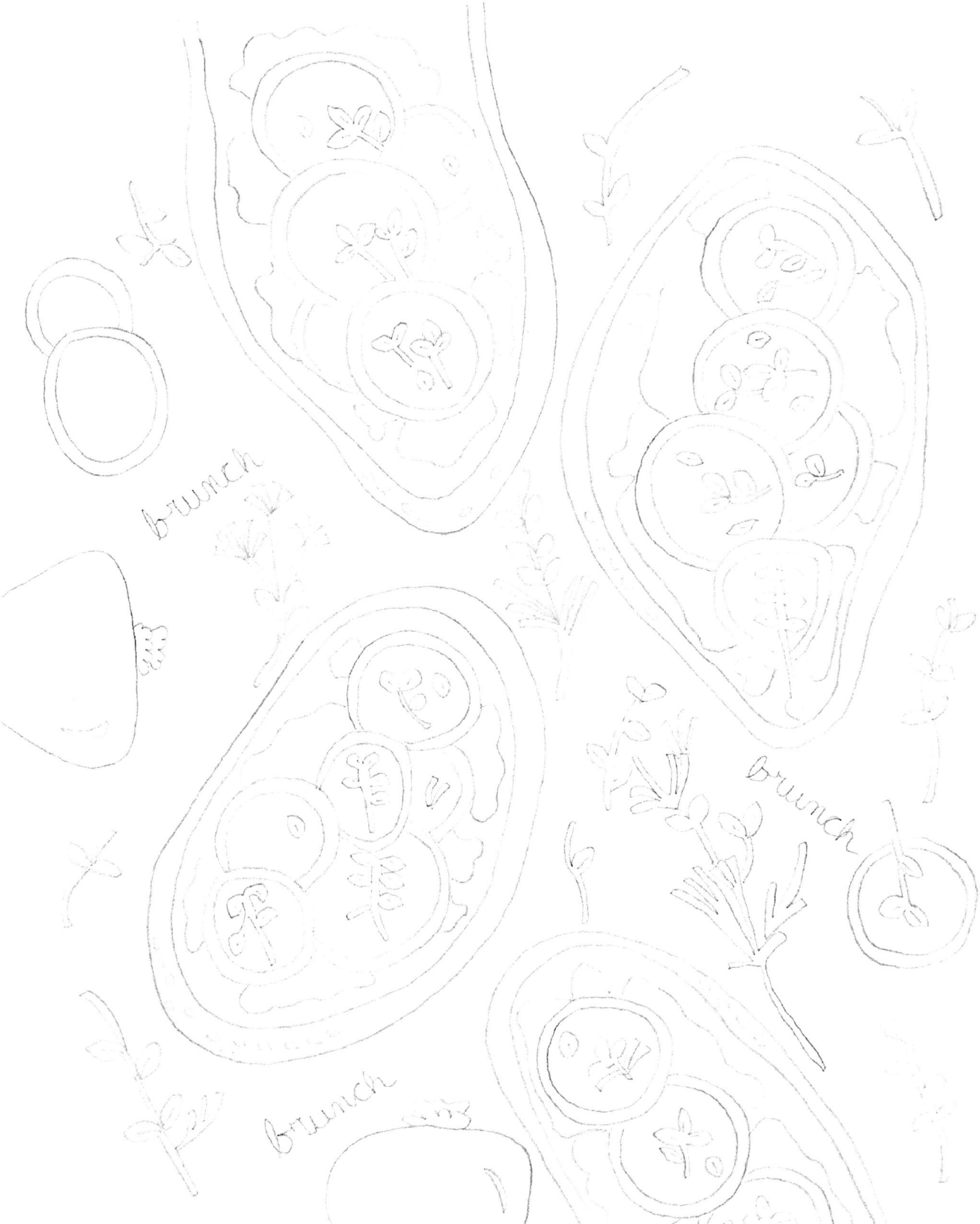
brunch
brunch
brunch

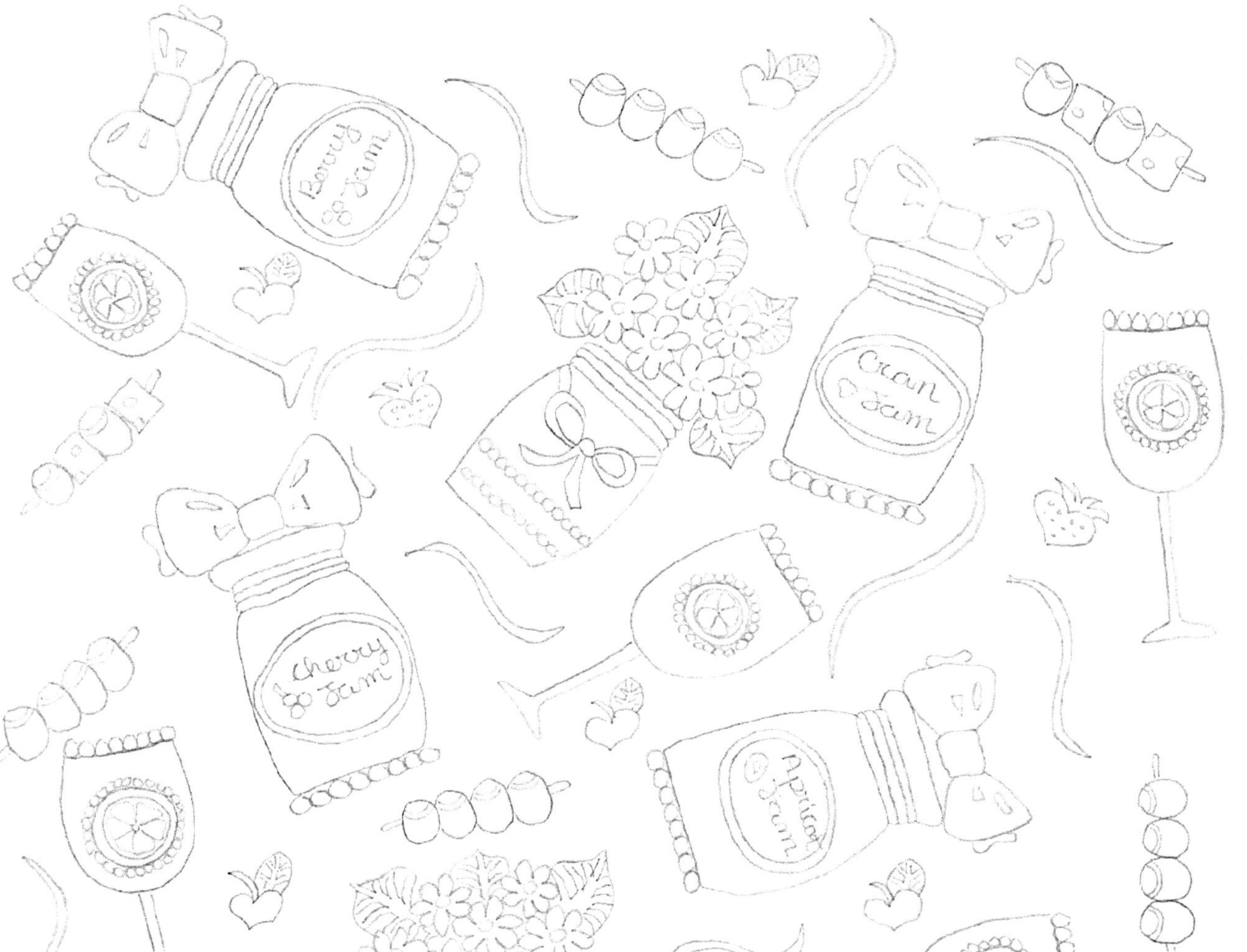
Berry Jam
Cran Jam
Cherry Jam
Apricot Jam
Apple Jam
Grape Jam

wine
Garden
Garden
Vintage
Garden
wine
wine
Vintage
Garden
Vintage
Vintage
wine
Garden
wine

you had
me at
merlot

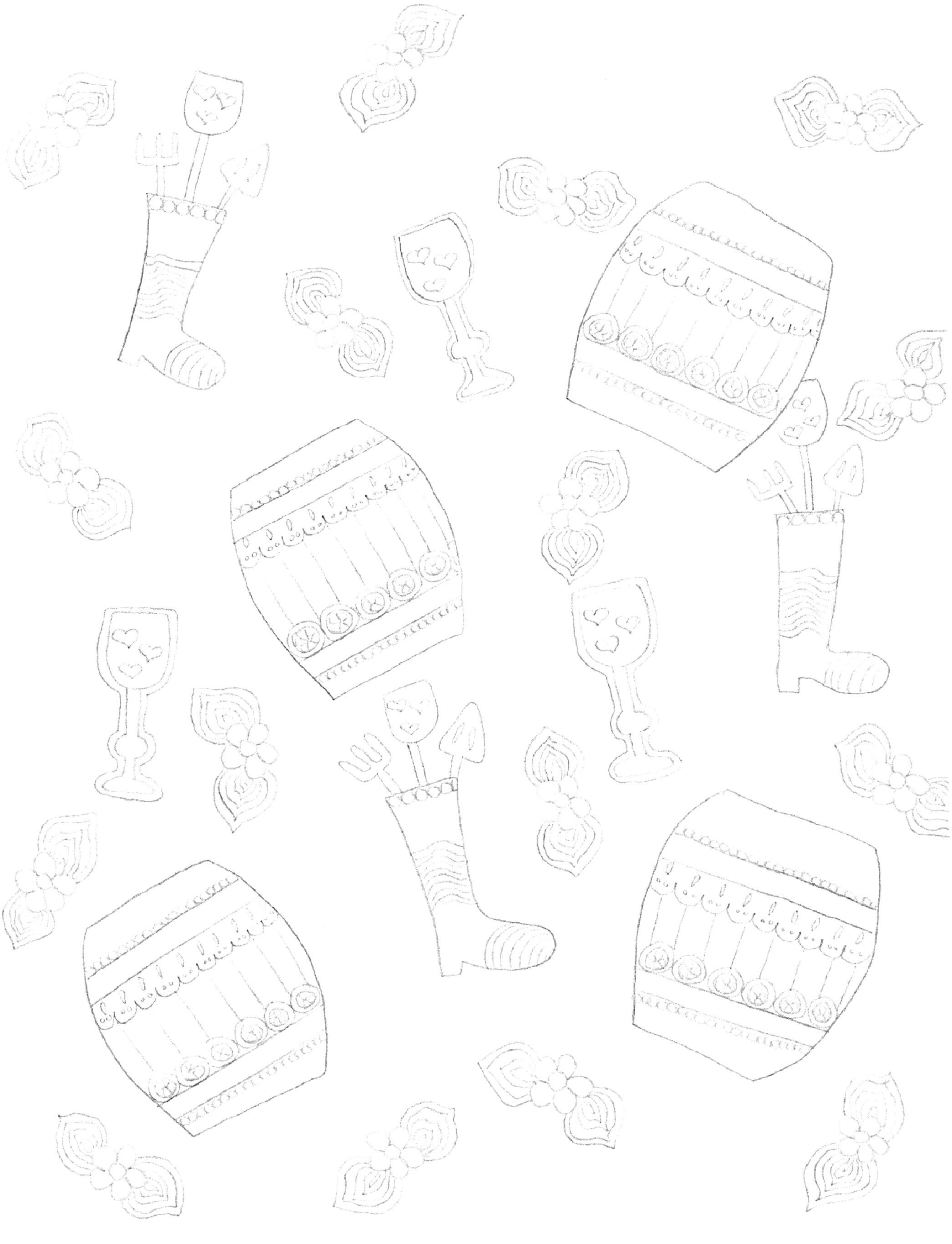

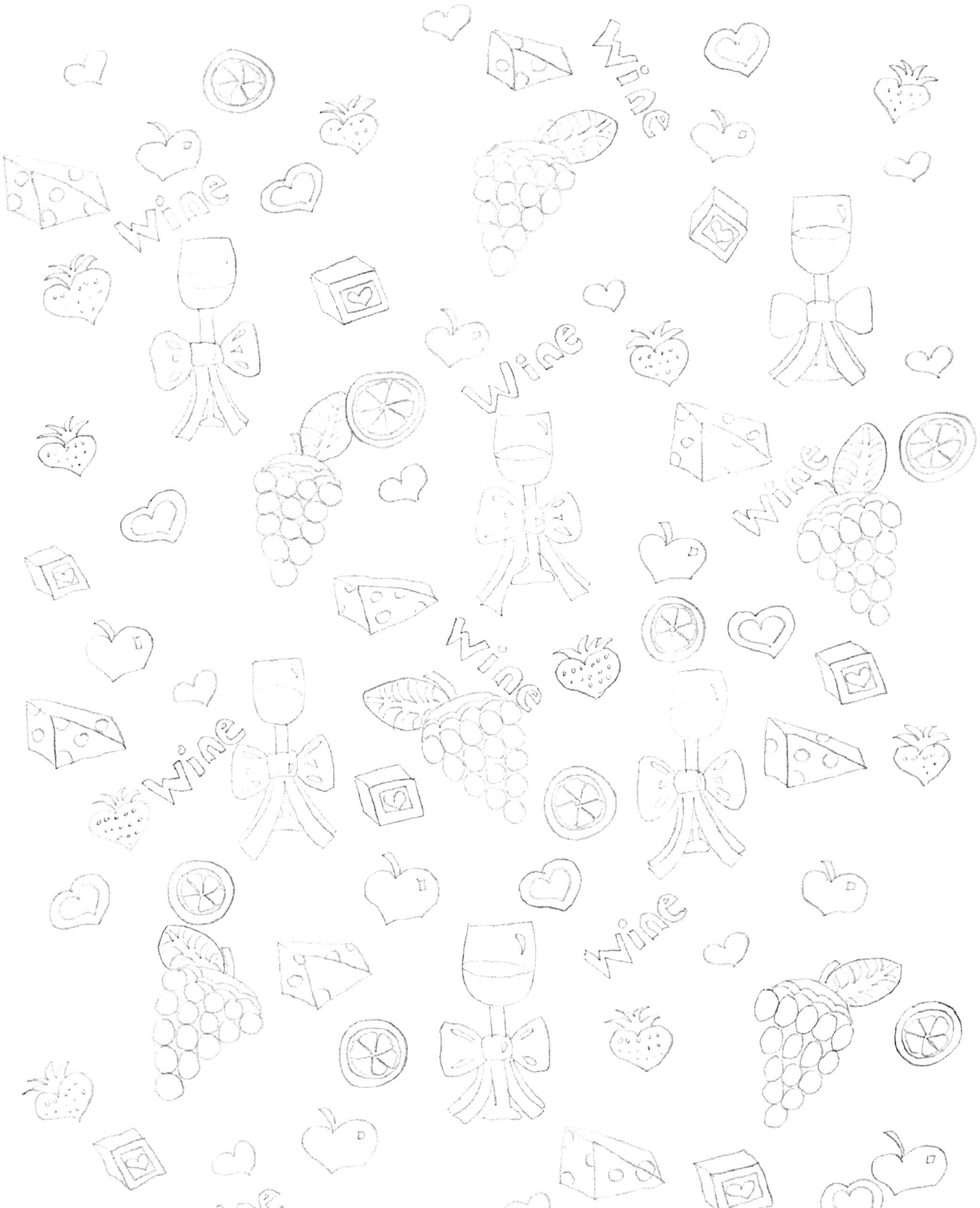
Wine
Wine
Wine
Wine
Wine
Wine
Wine
Wine

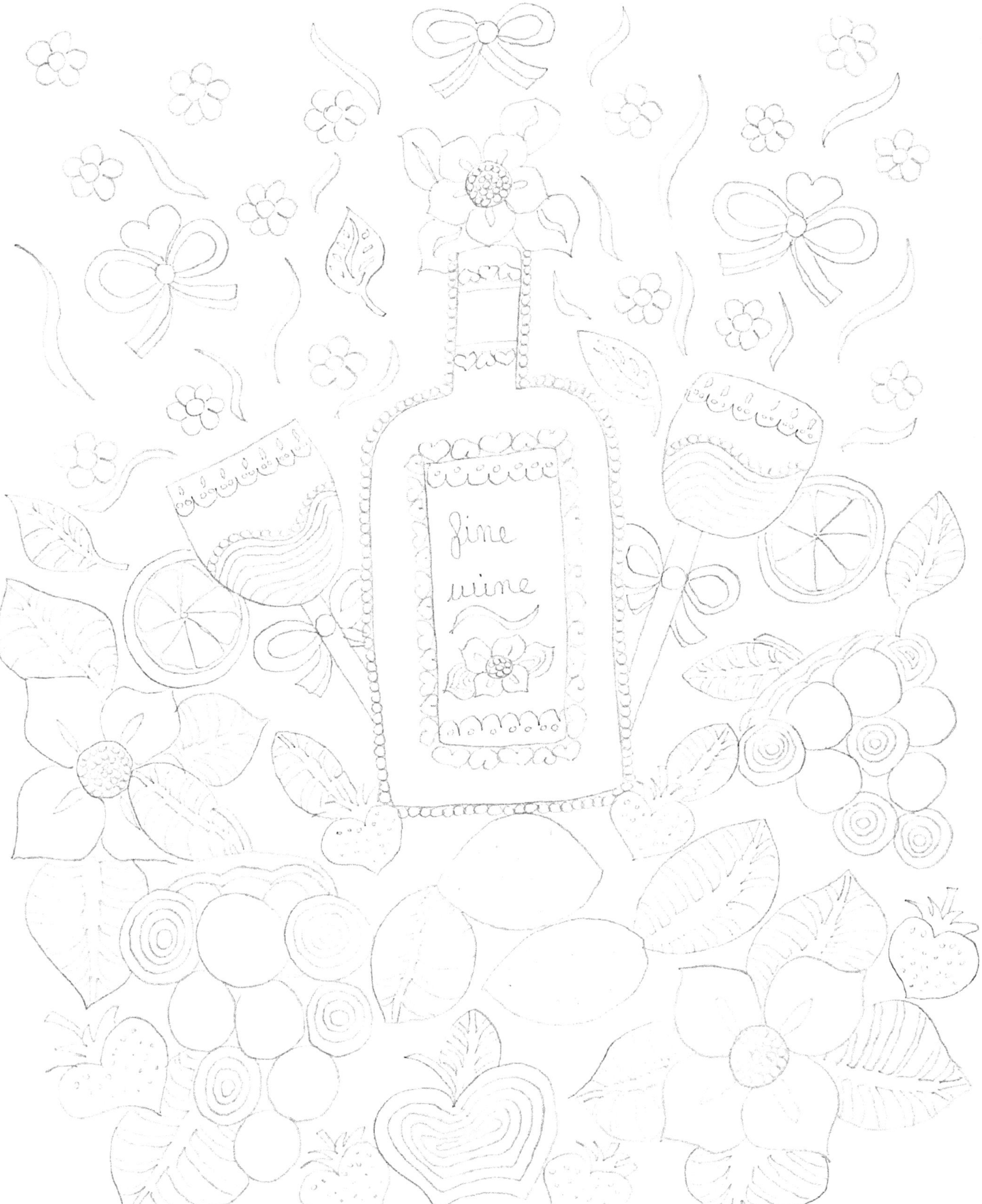
fine wine

wine
wine
wine
wine
wine

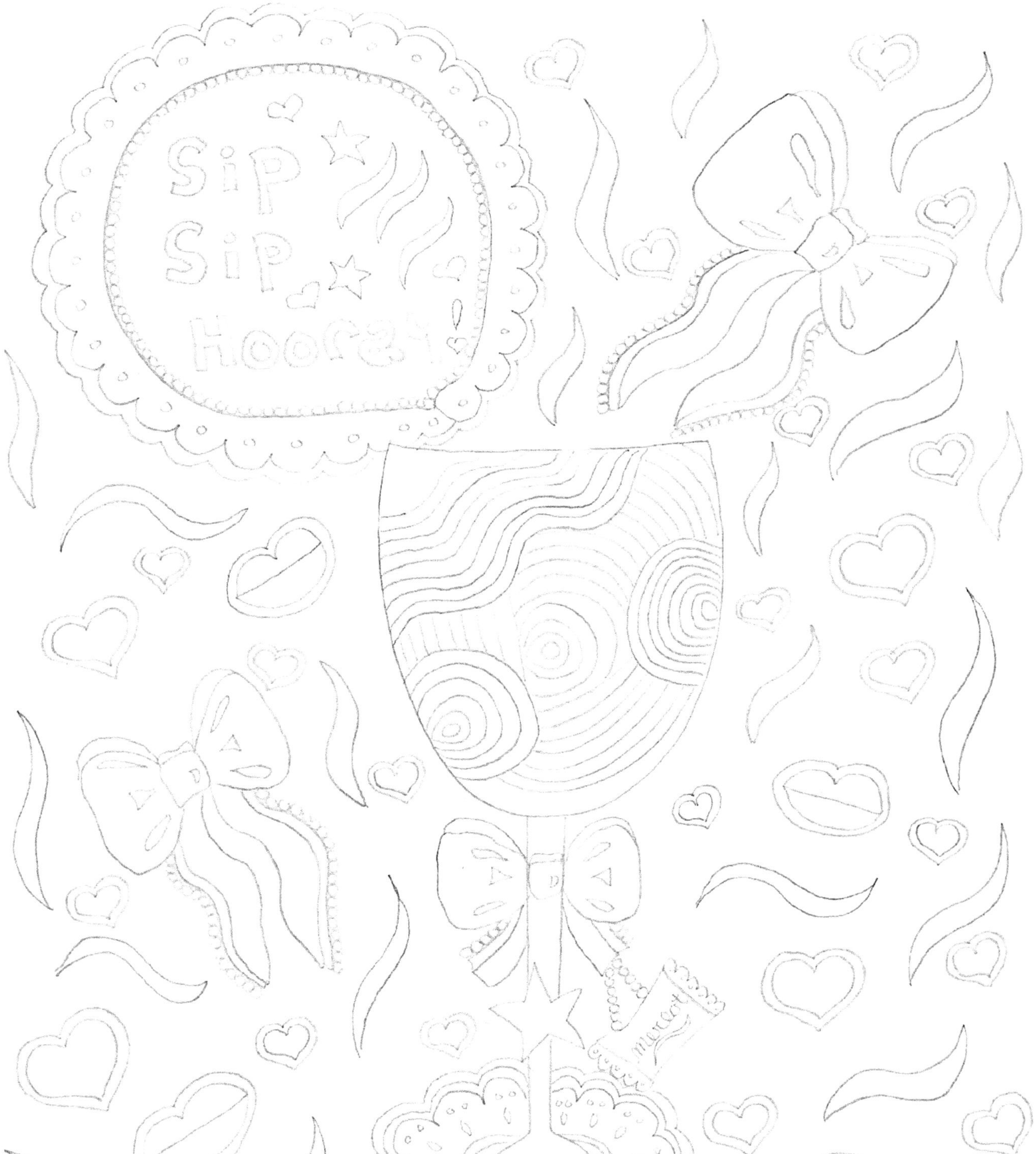
Sip Sip Hooray!

www.ingramcontent.com/pod-product-compliance
Lightning Source LLC
Chambersburg PA
CBHW082014230526
45468CB00022B/2224
* 9 7 8 1 7 2 1 1 4 5 5 0 8 *